150
Essential MCQs
for Surgical Finals

PASTEST

Dedicated to your success

150 Essential MCQs for Surgical Finals

Delilah Hassanally BSc MBBS MSc FRCS
*Surgical Trainee, St Helier's Hospital,
Carshalton, Surrey*

Rema Singh BA MBBS MA MRCP
*Specialist Registrar in Radiology,
Addenbrooke's Hospital, Cambridge*

©1997 PASTEST
Egerton Court, Parkgate Estate,
Knutsford, Cheshire, UK
Telephone: 01565 752000

First published 1997
Reprinted 1999, 2001

ISBN: 1 901198 01 4

A catalogue record for this book is available from the British Library.

Typeset by EDITEXT, Charlesworth, High Peak, Derbyshire.
Printed by JW Arrowsmith Ltd., Bristol.

CONTENTS

Introduction   vii
MCQ Examination Technique   viii
Sample Answer Sheet   x
Revision Checklist   xi
Operations Checklist   xiv
Abbreviations   xv
Normal Ranges   xvii

MULTIPLE CHOICE QUESTION PAPER 1   1
    Answer Sheet   18
    Teaching Notes   19

MULTIPLE CHOICE QUESTION PAPER 2   55
    Answer Sheet   72
    Teaching Notes   73

MULTIPLE CHOICE QUESTION PAPER 3   105
    Answer Sheet   122
    Teaching Notes   123

Recommended Reading List   152
Revision Index   153
PasTest Revision Books   157

MORE BOOKS FOR MEDICAL STUDENTS
FROM PASTEST

PasTest are the specialists in study guides and revision courses for professional medical qualifications. For 25 years we have been helping doctors to achieve their potential. The new PasTest range of books for medical students includes:

OSCEs for Medical Undergraduates — Volume 1
  Feather, Visvanathan & Lumley (ISBN 1 901198 04 9)
OSCEs for Medical Undergraduates — Volume 2
  Visvanathan, Feather & Lumley (ISBN 1 901198 05 7)
● *Cover history-taking, examinations, investigations practical techniques, making a diagnosis, prescribing treatment and other issues*
● *Each chapter includes questions from each type of OSCE station*

Surgical Finals: Passing the Clinical
  Kuperberg & Lumley (ISBN 0 906896 38 X)
Medical Finals: Passing the Clinical
  Moore & Richardson (ISBN 0 906896 43 6)
● 100 typical long and short clinical cases
● Syllabus checklists for systematic revision
● Structured examination plans for all cases

Surgical Finals: Structured Answer & Essay Questions
  Visvanathan & Lumley (ISBN 0 906896 69 X)
Medical Finals: Structured Answer & Essay Questions
  Feather, Visvanathan & Lumley (ISBN 0 906896 79 7)
● Unique combination of essay questions and the new SAQs
● Sample essays and model essay plans
● Revision checklists to track your progress

150 Essential MCQs for Surgical Finals
  Hassanally & Singh (ISBN 1 901198 01 4)
150 Essential MCQs for Medical Finals
  Singh & Hassanally (ISBN 1 901198 02 2)
● The crucial material for your exam success
● Extended teaching notes, bullet points and mnemonics
● Revision indexes for easy access to specific topics

For further details contact PasTest on

Freephone 0800 980 9814

PasTest, Freepost, Knutsford, Cheshire WA16 7BR, UK
Fax: 01565 650624
E-mail: enquiries@pastest.co.uk
Web site: http://www.pastest.co.uk

INTRODUCTION

There are many multiple choice question books for postgraduate medical examinations, and for years undergraduates preparing for finals have been forced to struggle with these as there is very little revision material specific to their needs.

The aim of this book is to provide 'real' MCQ practice examinations at the appropriate level for undergraduates sitting their final surgical examinations. These questions will also benefit those sitting the PLAB examination.

This book contains three test papers designed to be similar in format, content and balance of subjects to surgical finals MCQ examinations. Answers and detailed teaching notes are given for each question. The questions are as 'real' as possible; they include material that has been remembered by medical students after their surgical finals examination.

There is a natural tendency to recall the harder and more confusing topics, but rather than avoiding these, we have deliberately included them and so the pass mark for each paper is probably a little less than 50%. We hope medical students will use this to their advantage; everyone will get the easy questions right, but the medical student who enters the examination having done the more difficult questions should not just pass, but pass well.

Delilah Hassanally
Rema Singh

Acknowledgement

The authors would like to thank Mr S Elsmore FRCS, Higher Surgical Trainee, St Helier's Hospital, Carshalton, Surrey for his help and encouragement.

Before sitting an MCQ examination, you will need to know how many questions are likely to be on the paper and how long you will be given to complete it. Thus you will be able to assess the approximate amount of time that can be spent on each question. Pacing yourself accurately during the examination to finish on time, or with time to spare, is essential.

In MCQ examinations you must read the question (both stem and items A–E) carefully. Take care not to mark the wrong boxes and think very carefully before making a mark on the answer sheet. Regard each option as being independent of every other item – each refers to a specific quantum of knowledge. The item (or the stem and the item taken together) make up a statement. You are required to indicate whether you regard this statement as 'True' or 'False'. Look only at a single statement when answering – disregard all the other statements presented in the question. They have nothing to do with the item you are concentrating on.

As you go through the questions, you can either mark your answers immediately on the answer sheet, or you can mark them on the question paper and then transfer them to the answer sheet. If you adopt the second approach, you must take great care not to make any errors and not to run out of time, since you will not be allowed extra time to transfer marks to the answer sheet. The answer sheet must always be marked neatly and carefully according to the instructions given. Careless marking is probably one of the commonest causes of rejection of answer sheets by the document reader.

- Do as many good quality practice papers as possible. This will help you to identify your strengths and weaknesses in time for further study. You can also use the Revision Index at the back of this book to find questions on specific topics, so that after you can done some reading you can test your knowledge

- With the three exams provided in this book be strict with yourself and work under realistic exam conditions. You should develop an understanding of your own work rate so that you know how much time you can spend on each question.

- Read each question several times. Nobody at this vital stage in their career should be wasting marks because they misread or misunderstood the question.

● Each exam in this book contains 50 questions.

● If you have to guess the answer to a question, put a special mark next to it. You will then be able to find out if you are a good guesser. This is especially important if your examination is negatively marked, i.e. marks will be deducted for incorrect answers. It is important to *know* what you know as well as what you don't know!

● Use the Revision Checklist on the following pages to keep a record of the subjects you have covered and feel confident about. This will ensure that you do not miss out any key topics.

MCQ ANSWER SHEET

UNIVERSITY OF LONDON Management Systems Division

MULTIPLE-CHOICE EXAMINATION ANSWER SHEET

	Candidate No.	Test No.	College No.

DATE.................

SURNAME.................

FIRST NAME(S).................

Instructions: Use the HB pencil provided. To make an answer draw a single horizontal line along the dotted line **above** the appropriate letter or number. To answer 'TRUE' draw your line **above** the capital letter in the upper row. To answer 'FALSE' draw your line **above** the lower case letter in the lower row. For example:

[A] for 'TRUE'   [A] for 'FALSE'
[a]   [a]

If you change your mind and wish to cancel a completed answer, draw another line **below** the letter or number, along the dotted line. **Do not rub out.**

Candidate No.: [0][0][0][0] [1][1][1][1] [2][2][2][2] [3][3][3][3] [4][4][4][4] [5][5][5][5] [6][6][6][6] [7][7][7][7] [8][8][8][8] [9][9][9][9]

Test No.: [θ][0][0][0] [1][1][1][1] [P][2][2][2] [3][3][3] [4][4][4] [5][5][5] [6][6][6] [7][7][7] [8][8][8] [9][9][9]

College No.: [0][0] [1][1] [2][2] [3][3] [4][4] [5][5] [6][6] [7][7] [8][8] [9][9]

Shown below is the correct method of completion, the correct method of cancellation/alteration and examples of various incorrect methods of completion.

CORRECT METHOD OF COMPLETION

True = [A]   False = [A]
       [a]   [a]

CORRECT METHOD OF CANCELLATION/ALTERATION

To cancel a response, draw a line below the letter. Do not rub out. Thus:

[A] or [A] = Cancelled
[a]   [a]

To alter a response, first cancel. Then draw a line above the other letter. Thus:

False = [A]   True = [A]
        [a]   [a]

INCORRECT METHODS OF COMPLETION

Too faint [A]

Slanted [A]

Too low [A]

Too high [A]

Into next box [A][B]

Too short [A][A][A]

Isolated cancellation [A]

DETERMINATE TYPE T

Questions 1–60, each with answer options:

[A] [B] [C] [D] [E]
[a] [b] [c] [d] [e]

KENRICK&JEFFERSON   MP/20 3077 20M 8/95   Printers to the Computer Industry

Reproduced by kind permission of the University of London.

X

REVISION CHECKLIST

Use this checklist to record your revision progress. Tick the subjects when you feel confident that you have covered them adequately. This will ensure that you do not forget to revise any key topics. This list is arranged in approximate order of importance. Items closest to the top of each list are most likely to come up in examinations.

GASTROINTESTINAL SYSTEM – UPPER
- [ ] Acid reflux
- [ ] Peptic ulcer
- [ ] Achalasia
- [ ] Upper GI bleed
- [ ] Small bowel obstruction
- [ ] Mesenteric embolus
- [ ] Crohn's disease
- [ ] Post-gastrectomy symptoms
- [ ] Oesophageal malignancy
- [ ] Paralytic ileus
- [ ] Pancreatitis; pancreatic tumours
- [ ] Acute appendicitis
- [ ] Hernias – femoral and inguinal
- [ ] Parotid tumours
- [ ] Carcinoma of the tongue
- [ ] Barium studies; endoscopy

GASTROINTESTINAL SYSTEM – LOWER
- [ ] Inflammatory bowel disease
- [ ] Diverticular disease
- [ ] Malignancy
- [ ] Fistulae
- [ ] Haemorrhoids
- [ ] Anal fissure
- [ ] Pilonidal abscess

HEPATOBILIARY SYSTEM
- [ ] Gallstones
- [ ] Cholecystitis
- [ ] Ascending cholangitis
- [ ] Jaundice
- [ ] Radiological procedures, for example, ERCP and PTC

☐ Hepatitis B
☐ Hydatid cyst of the liver

VASCULAR
Venous –
☐   varicose veins
☐   deep vein thrombosis
Arterial –
☐   ischaemia
☐   carotid stenosis
☐   peripheral vascular disease

RENAL SYSTEM
☐ Neoplasia
☐ Calculi
☐ Acute renal failure
☐ Investigations, for example, intravenous urography

UROGENITAL TRACT
☐ Testicular tumours
☐ Scrotal swellings
☐ Varicocele
☐ Hydrocele
☐ Undescended testes

TRAUMA
☐ Chest
☐ Spleen
☐ Kidney
☐ Head injury

SKIN
☐ Malignant melanoma
☐ Carbuncle
☐ Basal cell carcinoma

NERVOUS SYSTEM
☐ Horner's syndrome
☐ Bell's palsy

MISCELLANEOUS

- [ ] Breast – benign and malignant lesions
- [ ] Thyroid – cystic and solid swellings
- [ ] Post-operative complications
- [ ] Wound healing
- [ ] Fluid replacement
- [ ] Shock/hypovolaemia

OPERATIONS CHECKIST

Medical students need to be aware of certain operations which are performed routinely. This short list is by no means comprehensive, but can be used as a guideline. You need to know the indication for the operation and basic principles regarding pre- and post-operative management. There is no need for detailed knowledge on the procedure itself. Use this list to tick off the procedures when you feel confident of your knowledge.

GASTROINTESTINAL TRACT
☐ Oesophagectomy
☐ Billorth I and II (Polya) gastrectomy
☐ Small bowel resection
☐ Appendicectomy
☐ Hemicolectomy, subtotal colectomy, stomas
☐ Hartmann's procedure
☐ Anterior resection and abdomino-perineal resection of the rectum
☐ Haemorrhoidectomy
☐ Lateral sphincterotomy

VASCULAR
☐ Carotid endarterectomy
☐ Femoral-politeal artery bypass graft
☐ High saphenous ligation and stripping of the long saphenous vein

BREAST
☐ Lumpectomy
☐ Mastectomy

THYROID
☐ Lobectomy, total thyroidectomy

UROLOGY
☐ Transurethral resection of the prostate (TURP)
☐ Nephrectomy

OTHERS
☐ Laparoscopic cholecystectomy
☐ Lichtenstein repair of inguinal hernias
☐ Nissen's fundoplication for hiatus hernia

ABBREVIATIONS

ACTH	Adrenocorticotrophin hormone
ADH	Antidiuretic hormone
APTT	Activated partial thromboplastin time
ARDS	Acute respiratory distress syndrome
AXR	Abdominal X-ray
BR	Serum bilirubin
CT	Computerized tomography
CVP	Central venous pressure
DNA	Deoxyribonucleic acid
DVT	Deep vein thrombosis
E. coli	Escherichia coli
EBV	Epstein–Barr virus
ECG	Electrocardiogram
ERCP	Endoscopic retrograde cholangiopancreatography
ESR	Erythrocyte sedimentation rate
GOJ	Gastro-oesophageal junction
H^+	Hydrogen ion
HCl	Hydrochloric acid
INR	Internalized ratio
IVU	Intravenous urogram
K^+	Potassium ion
KUB	Kidney, ureter and bladder
Na^+	Sodium ion
NaCl	Sodium chloride
NGT	Nasogastric tube
NSAIDs	Non-steroidal anti-inflammatory drugs
OGD	Oesophagogastroduodenoscopy
pCO_2	Partial pressure of carbon dioxide
PEG	Percutaneous endoscopic gastrostomy

PTC	Percutaneous transhepatic cholangiogram
PVD	Peripheral vascular disease
RNA	Ribonucleic acid
TB	Tuberculosis
TPN	Total parenteral nutrition
USS	Ultrasound scan

NORMAL RANGES

Serum	Normal Range
Albumin	36–52 g/l
Amylase	70–300 iu/l
Bicarbonate	22–28 mmol/l
Bilirubin	5–20 μmol/l
Calcium	2.20–2.60 mmol/l
Chloride	95–105 mmol/l
Creatinine kinase	23–175 iu/l
Creatinine	60–120 μmol/l
Gammaglutaryltransferase (GGT)	<40 iu/l
Globulins	24–37 g/l

Immunoglobulins

IgG	5.3–16.5 g/l
IgA	0.8–4.0 g/l
IgM	0.5–2.0 g/l
Iron	14–29 μmol/l
Iron binding capacity (TIBC)	45–75 μmol/l
Lactate dehydrogenase (LDH)	100–300 iu/l
Magnesium	0.70–1.00 mmol/l
Osmolarity	270–295 mmol/l
Phosphatase (acid)	0–4 iu/l
Phosphatase (alkaline)	40–115 iu/l
Phosphate	0.8–1.4 mmol/l
Potassium	3.5–5.0 mmol/l
Protein	62–82 g/l
Sodium	135–145 mmol/l

Thyroid function tests

T_4	54–144 nmol/l
TSH	0.10–5.0 mU/l

T_3	0.8–2.7 nmol/l
FT_4	9–25 pmol/l
TBG	10–30 mg/l
Transaminase ALT	11–55 iu/l
Transaminase AST	13–42 iu/l
Transferrin	2–4 g/l
Urate	0.24–0.45 mmol/l
Urea	2.5–6.6 mmol/l

PLASMA

Glucose	3.0–5.9 mmol/l
Arterial blood gases	
[H⁺]	36–43 nmol/l
pCO_2	4.6–6.0 kPa
[HCO_3]	20–28 mmol/l
pO_2	10.5–13.5 kPa
Lactate	0.63–2.44 mmol/l
Pyruvate	34–80 µmol/l

CEREBROSPINAL FLUID (CSF)

Glucose	2.5–3.9 mmol/l
Protein	<0.45 g/l

URINE

Catecholamines	<1.3 µmol/24 h
VMA (HMMA)	9–36 µmol/24 h
5HIAA	10–50 µmol/24 h
Microalbumin	<30 mg/l
Creatinine clearance	60–110 ml/min

MISCELLANEOUS

Faecal fat	<10 mmol/24 h
Xylose excretion test	
Urine excretion (25 g dose)	>33 mmol/5 h
Urine excretion (5 g dose)	>8 mmol/5 h
Blood xylose at 1 h (25 g dose)	2.0–4.8 mmol/l
Blood xylose at 2 h (25 g dose)	1.0–5.0 mmol/l

50 questions: time allowed 2 hours.
Mark your answers with a tick (True) or a cross (False) in
the box provided. Leave the box blank for 'Don't know'.
Do not look at the answers until you have completed the
whole question paper.

1.1 The following refer to hiatus hernia:

☐ A the treatment of choice is fundoplication   F
☐ B rolling hernias are more common than the sliding F
     type
☐ C severe acid reflux occurs mainly in rolling hernias F
☐ D it can be diagnosed by endoscopy   T
☐ E weight loss is advised   T

1.2 Perforated duodenal ulcer

☐ A may be treated conservatively   T
☐ B should be confirmed by gastroscopy before   F
     laparotomy
☐ C should be confirmed by CT before laparotomy   F
☐ D can present without abdominal signs   T
☐ E is excluded if the serum amylase is more than
     500 SI units/l   F

1.3 Duke's staging of colo-rectal carcinoma

☐ A involves assessment of lymph node spread T
☐ B requires assessment of the depth of tumour T
     penetration through the wall of the bowel
☐ C involves assessment of the presence or absence of
     metastases in distant organs   F
☐ D is made at post-mortem   F
☐ E requires measurement of the distances between the
     tumour and the resection lines   T

1.4 Ulcerative colitis

☐ A may be complicated by retinitis
☐ B should be investigated by rectal biopsy
☐ C may predispose to carcinoma of the large bowel especially with the early onset of total colitis
☐ D should be investigated by colonoscopy if there is dilation of the large bowel on plain X-ray
☐ E is not associated commonly with protein loss

1.5 Common causes of small bowel obstruction in adults are

☐ A stricture due to ulcerative colitis
☐ B adhesions
☐ C Meckel's diverticulum
☐ D intussusception
☐ E strangulated hernia

1.6 Recognized consequences of achalasia of the cardia include

☐ A dysphagia
☐ B pneumonia
☐ C carcinoma of the oesophagus
☐ D absent gastric air bubble
☐ E heartburn

1.7   First-degree haemorrhoids are a cause of

☐   A rectal bleeding
☐   B anal pain
☐   C rectal mucosal prolapse
☐   D melaena
☐   E *pruritis ani*

1.8   Femoral hernia

☐   A frequently becomes strangulated
☐   B is more common in men than in women
☐   C causes swelling of the lower limb
☐   D may be confused with an enlarged lymph node
☐   E is more common than inguinal hernia

1.9   Endoscopic retrograde cholangiopancreatography (ERCP)

☐   A usually requires general anaesthetic
☐   B is valuable for confirming a suspicion of acute pancreatitis
☐   C gives information equivalent to that obtained by percutaneous transhepatic cholangiography
☐   D is contraindicated in the presence of jaundice
☐   E can diagnose strictures of the pancreatic duct

1.10 Gallstones

- ☐ A are usually formed in the bile ducts
- ☐ B have been found in the stools
- ☐ C are causally related to carcinoma of the gallbladder
- ☐ D are usually radio-opaque
- ☐ E can cause acute pancreatitis

1.11 Typical biochemical features of serum in obstructive jaundice include

- ☐ A raised bilirubin
- ☐ B increased acid phosphatase
- ☐ C increased alkaline phosphatase
- ☐ D increased amylase
- ☐ E hepatitis B surface antigen

1.12 Splenectomy is likely to be of value in

- ☐ A congenital spherocytosis
- ☐ B myelofibrosis
- ☐ C malaria
- ☐ D infectious mononucleosis
- ☐ E agranulocytosis

1.13 A lump in the midline of the neck may be

- ☐ A a dermoid cyst
- ☐ B a sebaceous cyst
- ☐ C a thyroglossal cyst
- ☐ D a branchial cyst
- ☐ E a cystic hygroma

1.14 Carcinoma of the breast may present with

- ☐ A peau d'orange
- ☐ B shortness of breath
- ☐ C lymphoedema of the arm
- ☐ D a fracture of bone
- ☐ E inversion of the nipple

1.15 In ureteric obstruction due to a calculus, an intravenous urogram would be expected to show

- ☐ A normal function in the non-affected kidney
- ☐ B delayed function in the affected kidney
- ☐ C swelling of the affected kidney
- ☐ D contraction of the unaffected kidney
- ☐ E extravasation of contrast from the renal pelvis

1.16 A size 24 Fr catheter

- ☐ A must always be inserted using aseptic technique
- ☐ B is 24 mm in diameter
- ☐ C is 24 mm in length
- ☐ D is 24 mm in external circumference
- ☐ E is the suitable first choice for urethral catheterization of the adult male

1.17 Renal carcinoma in adults

- ☐ A usually presents as painful haematuria
- ☐ B commonly metastasizes to bone
- ☐ C may grow into the inferior vena cava
- ☐ D may give rise to a cannon ball metastasis
- ☐ E is called a Wilms' tumour

1.18 A patient has a road traffic accident resulting in severe chest injury. He presents in severe respiratory distress and his trachea is deviated to the left. The first thing you should do is to

- ☐ A order an urgent X-ray
- ☐ B insert an exploratory needle into the second left intercostal space
- ☐ C perform an emergency tracheostomy
- ☐ D gain intravenous access
- ☐ E obtain an electrocardiogram

1.19 A full thickness burn of the right leg

- ☐ A is estimated to be 5% of the entire body surface area
- ☐ B may cause a peptic ulcer
- ☐ C may result in thrombosis
- ☐ D is treated by resuscitation with intravenous fluids
- ☐ E should be covered with ice

1.20 Varicose veins

- ☐ A cause lipodermatosclerosis
- ☐ B should always be treated by injection sclerotherapy
- ☐ C are common in rural Africa
- ☐ D are more common in the short than in the long saphenous system
- ☐ E can cause serious haemorrhage

1.21 Intermittent claudication

- ☐ A is usually caused by atherosclerosis
- ☐ B is worse at night
- ☐ C may improve on continued exercise
- ☐ D may proceed to gangrene
- ☐ E requires surgery to the affected arteries

1.22 Clinical features of acute pancreatitis include

- ☐ A tetany
- ☐ B paralytic ileus
- ☐ C vomiting
- ☐ D jaundice
- ☐ E a pleural effusion

1.23 Symptoms of malignant change in a melanoma are

- ☐ A bleeding
- ☐ B hair in the lesion
- ☐ C change in colour
- ☐ D itching
- ☐ E satellite lesions

1.24 A fistula

- ☐ A arises from a blind ending abscess cavity
- ☐ B will never heal spontaneously
- ☐ C connects two separate epithelial surfaces
- ☐ D may be found in the anal canal
- ☐ E may give rise to severe fluid and electrolyte losses

1.25 Normal saline given intravenously

☐   A   is a solution containing one mole of sodium chloride per litre of water

☐   B   is a solution containing 0.9 g of sodium chloride per litre of water

☐   C   has the same osmotic pressure as plasma

☐   D   is a 0.9% solution of sodium chloride in water

☐   E   should never be given for hypovolaemia

1.26 In patients with chronic vomiting

☐   A   a metabolic acidosis results

☐   B   a metabolic alkalosis results

☐   C   there is excess loss of sodium in the urine

☐   D   potassium deficiency may occur

☐   E   there may be the same metabolic effect as continual nasogastric aspiration

1.27 Factors which favour wound healing include

☐   A   a good blood supply

☐   B   a haematoma

☐   C   tension

☐   D   the presence of bacteria

☐   E   a minimum of suture materials

1.28 Causes of hypotension in adults include

- ☐ A an upper gastrointestinal bleed
- ☐ B intracranial bleeding
- ☐ C myocardial infarction
- ☐ D infarction of the small bowel
- ☐ E systemic infection with Gram-negative organisms

1.29 Nutritional problems seen after a partial gastrectomy include

- ☐ A macrocytic anaemia
- ☐ B osteoporosis
- ☐ C weight loss
- ☐ D iron deficiency anaemia
- ☐ E hypoglycaemia

1.30 Subphrenic abscesses

- ☐ A are best treated by antibiotics
- ☐ B occur after perforated peptic ulcer
- ☐ C may be associated with a pleural effusion on the same side
- ☐ D cause hiccoughs
- ☐ E should not be treated by aspiration alone

1.31 The following are features of Horner's syndrome:

☐ A dilatation of the ipsilateral pupil
☐ B enophthalmos
☐ C absent sweating on the affected side of the face
☐ D deviation of the tongue to one side on protrusion
☐ E ptosis of the ipsilateral eye

1.32 Clinical features typical of acute appendicitis include

☐ A *fetor oris*
☐ B fever
☐ C pain in the right shoulder
☐ D guarding in the left iliac fossa
☐ E anorexia

1.33 In Bell's palsy

☐ A patients may complain of impairment of taste
☐ B there is unilateral facial weakness
☐ C there is unilateral loss of sensation of the skin
☐ D *Herpes zoster* is the cause
☐ E the voice is hoarse

1.34 Tearing of the medial meniscus of the knee leads to

- ☐ A quadriceps wasting
- ☐ B recurrent haemarthrosis
- ☐ C limitation of knee flexion
- ☐ D locking of the knee
- ☐ E intermittent effusions

1.35 Avascular necrosis occurs in

- ☐ A fracture through the waist of the scaphoid
- ☐ B dislocation of the lunate bone
- ☐ C subcapital fracture of the femoral neck
- ☐ D steroid therapy
- ☐ E caisson disease

1.36 Neuromuscular blocking agents that act by competitive inhibition include

- ☐ A pethidine
- ☐ B suxamethonium
- ☐ C neostigmine
- ☐ D hexamethonium
- ☐ E tubocurarine

1.37 Carcinoma of the stomach is associated with

☐   A   blood group O
☐   B   cigarette smoking
☐   C   pernicious anaemia
☐   D   iron deficiency anaemia
☐   E   transcoelomic spread to the ovary

1.38 Minimally invasive surgery

☐   A   is used for cholecystectomy
☐   B   affords a quicker recovery than open procedures
☐   C   can be used for cervical sympathectomy
☐   D   is contraindicated in morbid obesity
☐   E   means minimal skill is required

1.39 A sarcoma

☐   A   is a malignant tumour
☐   B   spreads primarily via the blood stream
☐   C   responds to radiotherapy
☐   D   grows rapidly
☐   E   has a good prognosis

1.40 Carcinoma of the prostate

- ☐ A occurs frequently in men over the age of 65 years
- ☐ B responds to testosterone therapy
- ☐ C can cause a rectal stricture
- ☐ D produces osteosclerotic secondary bone deposits
- ☐ E spreads to pelvic lymph nodes

1.41 The following classically occur within 24 hours of an operation:

- ☐ A deep vein thrombosis
- ☐ B pulmonary embolus
- ☐ C pulmonary atelectasis
- ☐ D retention of urine
- ☐ E reactionary haemorrhage

1.42 Gas gangrene is treated with

- ☐ A local applications of antiseptics
- ☐ B benzylpenicillin
- ☐ C adequate surgical excision of the wound
- ☐ D primary suture of the wound
- ☐ E blood transfusion

1.43 Fibroadenosis

- ☐   A   often produces cyclical pain
- ☐   B   is normally unilateral
- ☐   C   tends to progress in the post-menopausal years
- ☐   D   is pre-malignant
- ☐   E   produces diffuse lumpiness

1.44 Gynaecomastia occurs in

- ☐   A   carcinoma of the prostate
- ☐   B   chronic liver disease
- ☐   C   carcinoma of the breast
- ☐   D   peptic ulcer disease
- ☐   E   bronchial carcinoma

1.45 An abdominal aortic aneurysm

- ☐   A   may be seen on a plain abdominal X-ray
- ☐   B   may present with a collapsing pulse
- ☐   C   may be due to syphilis
- ☐   D   needs treatment only if it causes back pain
- ☐   E   usually involves the renal arteries

1.46 A nasogastric tube

☐   A   should be used to protect respiratory function in all patients with severe head injury

☐   B   should be spigotted and aspirated at regular intervals

☐   C   may be used for feeding

☐   D   is required in upper gastrointestinal bleeding to assess blood loss

☐   E   may be used in the treatment of large bowel obstruction

1.47 The following facts are true of pleomorphic adenomas:

☐   A   they occur in the parotid gland

☐   B   they are rapidly growing

☐   C   they can be safely removed by simple enucleation

☐   D   surgery may result in damage to the facial nerve

☐   E   surgery may result in Frey's syndrome

1.48 Which of the following conditions may predispose to the development of paralytic ileus:

☐   A   laparotomy

☐   B   potassium deficiency

☐   C   lumbar sympathectomy

☐   D   fracture of lumbar vertebrae

☐   E   calcium deficiency

1.49 Carcinoma of the oesophagus

☐ A occurs most frequently in the middle third of the oesophagus
☐ B is predominantly squamous in type
☐ C is a complication of oesophagitis
☐ D is associated with alcohol intake
☐ E occurs in Plummer–Vinson syndrome

1.50 In acute cholecystitis

☐ A immediate cholecystectomy may be performed
☐ B antibiotics are mandatory
☐ C delayed cholecystectomy may be performed
☐ D treatment includes laparoscopic cholecystectomy
☐ E laparotomy is advisable

──────────── **END** ────────────

**Go over your answers until your time is up.
Correct answers and teaching notes are overleaf.**

MULTIPLE CHOICE QUESTION PAPER 1 – ANSWERS

The correct answer options for each question are given below.

1.1	D E		1.26	B D E
1.2	A D		1.27	A E
1.3	A B		1.28	A C D E
1.4	B C		1.29	A C D E
1.5	B E		1.30	B C D
1.6	A B C D E		1.31	B C E
1.7	A E		1.32	A B E
1.8	A D		1.33	A B
1.9	E		1.34	A B C D E
1.10	B C E		1.35	A B C D E
1.11	A C		1.36	E
1.12	A B		1.37	B C D E
1.13	A B C		1.38	A B C
1.14	A B C D E		1.39	A B C D
1.15	A B C		1.40	A C D E
1.16	A		1.41	C D E
1.17	B C D		1.42	B C
1.18	None correct		1.43	A E
1.19	B C D		1.44	B E
1.20	A E		1.45	A C
1.21	A C D		1.46	C E
1.22	A B C D E		1.47	A D E
1.23	A C D E		1.48	A B D
1.24	C D E		1.49	A B D E
1.25	C D		1.50	A B C D

1.1 Hiatus hernia   Answers: D E

Hiatus hernia is classified into two types:

- Sliding – 90% are of this type. The gastro-oesopha-geal junction (GOJ) slides upwards into the thorax rendering it incompetent and results in acid reflux and its complications (see Paper 2, Question 1). Manage-ment of any surgical case involves conservative meas-ures, medical treatment and surgical intervention.

  Conservative measures include weight reduction (to decrease the intra-abdominal pressure), and raising the head of the bed.

  Medical treatment includes drugs such as H_2 antago-nists or proton pump inhibitors.

  The surgical treatment is Nissen's fundoplication. There are variations on this procedure but essentially the GOJ is pulled back into the abdomen and the fundus of the stomach is wrapped around it.

- Rolling (para-oesophageal) – 10% are of this type, commoner in obese females. The fundus of the stom-ach rotates in front of the oesophagus and herniates through the oesophageal hiatus up into the mediastinum. Note that the oesophageal sphincter is not affected and so reflux is not usually a problem. This type of hernia can be asymptomatic but occasion-ally the stomach can strangulate.

1.2 Perforated duodenal ulcer   Answers: A D

Perforation is an important complication of duodenal ulceration. It may present without abdominal signs particu-larly in the elderly and those on steroids. However, patients often present with peritonitis, the features of which are severe constant pain, rebound tenderness, guarding and rigidity and absent bowel sounds. Other important features are tachycardia, hypotension and pyrexia. Abnormal investigations include leucocytosis, raised amylase (not as high as in pancreatitis) and abnormal features on chest X-ray (gas under the diaphragm in 90%) and abdominal X-ray (bowel gas shadows).

Management may be conservative, for example, in the elderly or those unfit for surgery – symptomatic relief is provided whilst healing occurs as the omentum seals off the perforation. Surgery involves laparotomy with simple over-sewing of the perforation.

1.3 Duke's staging of colo-rectal cancer   Answers: A B

Duke's staging of colo-rectal cancer is made by pathological assessment of the affected bowel and its local lymph nodes. It is therefore not an assessment of distant spread. It is as follows:

- A: growth limited to the wall of colon (i.e. not through the serosa)
- B: extension through the wall and surrounding tissue but not to local lymph nodes
- C: metastases in the lymph nodes

Stage D has been used to describe Distant metastases but this was not part of the original classification. In general, staging of carcinoma is useful to predict prognosis and further management, for example, chemotherapy, radiotherapy, hormonal therapy, surgery.

In colo-rectal carcinoma, surgery may be curative for stage A; for stages B and C chemotherapy may be added.

The five-year survival after operation is as follows:

- Duke's A – 95%
- Duke's B – 70%
- Duke's C – 40%

Note that 50% of patients with colo-rectal cancer are incurable at presentation and therefore do not undergo radical surgery with the aim of cure. These patients die within five years.

1.4 Ulcerative colitis   **Answers: B C**

Ulcerative colitis is an inflammatory disorder of the mucosa and submucosa of the large bowel. It is often complicated by systemic features. These include anaemia (of chronic disease or of iron deficiency due to rectal bleeding), seronegative arthropathy (20%), uveitis and iritis, skin lesions (for example, erythema nodosum and pyoderma gangrenosum) and occasionally sclerosing cholangitis.

Specific investigations include:

- full blood count for anaemia, urea and electrolytes, ESR as a measure of disease activity, rectal examination followed by proctoscopy and sigmoidoscopy with a biopsy if necessary.
- abdominal X-ray may show colonic dilatation of toxic megacolon
- stool culture to exclude an infective cause
- contrast study – an urgent barium enema may be performed without bowel preparation, i.e. an 'instant enema' only if there is NO toxic dilatation on a plain film. This may show loss of haustrae, a lead pipe colon, or filling defects due to pseudopolyps or carcinoma.

- flexible colonoscopy – this is very useful to visualize bowel and permits excision of lesions such as polyps; it is used for surveillance, however, it carries the risk of perforation in fulminant cases of ulcerative colitis.

In young patients with total colitis for 10 years the risk of developing carcinoma of the colon or rectum is about 10%.

1.5 Small bowel obstruction   Answers: B E

Please read the question carefully. It is advisable to know a list of causes but beware of the question that has been altered slightly. The answers can often be worked out logically. In part 'A' the question refers to the small bowel and ulcerative colitis occurs in the large bowel!

Adhesions are a common cause of bowel obstruction.

Meckel's diverticulum is associated with a congenital band which may cause small bowel obstruction but this is not common (the commonest complication of Meckel's diverticulum is inflammation).

Intussusception is when a segment of bowel becomes invaginated into the bowel distal to it, i.e. 'telescoping'. It most commonly occurs in children but can sometimes occur in adults.

1.6 Achalasia   Answers: A B C D E

Achalasia is a disorder of oesophageal motility, resulting in contraction of the lower oesophageal sphincter. The proximal section becomes dilated. Patients are unable to tolerate both solids and fluids so that dysphagia is usually the presenting symptom. Fluids may spill over into the trachea causing an aspiration pneumonia. Vomiting and retrosternal pain may occur in severe cases. A chest X-ray will show a widened mediastinum and possibly a fluid level in the oesophagus. A barium swallow shows a 'beak' appearance with dilation of the oesophagus and a tapering constriction. The constriction prevents the passage of air into the stomach. There is an association between achalasia and oesophageal carcinoma.

1.7 **First-degree haemorrhoids**   **Answers: A E**
Haemorrhoids (piles) are abnormal dilated cushions of veins at the lower end of the anal mucosal columns. Symptoms of haemorrhoids include perianal irritation and itching (*pruritus ani*), pain, prolapse and bleeding. They are classified according to their position:

- first-degree haemorrhoids are not visible; they bleed after defecation and do not produce pain
- second-degree haemorrhoids prolapse after defecation, but then reduce spontaneously
- third-degree haemorrhoids prolapse and remain external
- fourth-degree haemorrhoids thrombose after prolapse.

Option C is false by definition. Haemorrhoids are usually located at the 3, 7, and 11 o'clock positions. They are situated above the dentate line and so can be injected painlessly.

Management is:

- conservative – high fibre diet, avoidance of straining and good anal hygiene

- medical – local anaesthetic agents, steroids and symptomatic relief
- surgical – submucosal injection, banding, and anal dilatation are used for first and second-degree haemorrhoids; haemorrhoidectomy is used for third or fourth-degree haemorrhoids.

1.8 Femoral hernia   Answers: A D

A femoral hernia is a passage of peritoneum and its contents (including fat or bowel) into the femoral canal. It is quite likely to become incarcerated or strangulated because the femoral canal/ring is narrow. The terms used vary but all have specific meanings, for example:

- irreducible – is self-explanatory
- obstructed – luminal contents obstructed but bowel is viable
- strangulated – blood supply is cut off; leads to infarction

Femoral hernias are more common in females than males, but in both sexes femoral hernias are less common than inguinal hernias. A femoral hernia arises below and lateral to the pubic tubercle. It is usually small. If it enlarges it tends to be deflected upwards. A cough impulse may not be detectable and therefore it may be difficult to distinguish from a lipoma or an enlarged lymph node.

1.9 Endoscopic retrograde cholangiopancreatography (ERCP)   Answer: E

Investigation of the biliary tree includes:

- abdominal X-ray (AXR) – only 10% of gallstones are radio-opaque

- ultrasound scan (USS) – is very useful to make the diagnosis of gallstones
- ERCP – used for imaging of the biliary tree and pancreatic ducts. It involves injection of contrast to outline the ducts. It allows the ampullary region of the pancreas to be inspected visually and the pancreatic duct may be outlined. It is helpful for identifying stones, strictures and tumours that cause obstruction as well as for therapeutic intervention, for example, stone extraction or stent insertion where there is a blockage. Endoscopic sphincterotomy can be performed. It is particularly useful in the jaundiced patient and in those patients who are unfit for surgery
- Percutaneous transhepatic cholangiography (PTC) – often used where ERCP fails, but it is more invasive. It involves entry via the skin into the liver and then injection of contrast into the duct system. There is no visual inflammation of the pancreas
- Cholangiography – this can be done operatively or via a T-tube.

1.10 Gallstones   **Answers: B C E**

Gallstones are almost always formed in the gallbladder (by precipitation from bile).They vary in content:

- ~5% are pigment stones
- ~20% are cholesterol stones
- ~75% contain both.

Pre-disposing factors include high concentration of bile, stasis and infection. Ninety per cent of stones are radiolucent. When a stone passes into the duodenum it may be found in the stool. Chronic inflammation of the gallbladder due to gallstones has been implicated in carcinoma of the gallbladder. Gallstones are present in most cases of gallbladder carcinoma. If a stone lodges in the ampulla of Vater it can cause acute pancreatitis. A stone lodged in the common bile duct can cause jaundice, ascending cholangitis or acute pancreatitis.

1.11 Obstructive jaundice   Answers: A C

In obstructive jaundice there is obstruction to bile drainage, preventing its normal flow into the duodenum. This is also known as extra-hepatic jaundice. As expected there is a rise in serum bilirubin (BR) and this is of the conjugated type as liver function is maintained. The urine appears dark as the excessive bilirubin is excreted by the kidney. The faeces are pale because of the lack of stercobilin which causes the brown colouration. (Note that urobilinogen is increased in urine in liver cell damage and haemolytic anaemia. It is initially colourless in urine but darkens on standing.)

In obstructive jaundice, liver function tests must be performed. Typically they show:

- bilirubin – raised
- alkaline phosphatase – raised (liver isoenzyme)
- transaminases – mild to moderate rise.

Acid phosphatase is raised in prostatic carcinoma. Amylase is a pancreatic enzyme which may or may not be raised in obstructive jaundice depending on the cause of the obstruction. It is by no means typical. Hepatitis B causes infective hepatitis resulting in liver damage and intrahepatic jaundice.

1.12 Spleen   Answers: A B

The spleen is a specialized lymphoid organ. It is highly vascular and is required for the maturation of white blood cells and for the destruction of effete red blood cells. Splenectomy is indicated for:

- hypersplenism/splenomegaly
- staging of lymphoma
- excision of tumours, cysts or abscesses.

Splenectomy may be useful in the following conditions:

- autoimmune thrombocytosis
- autoimmune haemolysis
- portal hypertension
- splenic vein hypertension
- Gaucher's disease
- myelofibrosis
- trauma.

Splenic rupture is an indication for splenectomy. This may be due to rib injuries, blunt trauma or peri-operative injury. Certain infections, such as Epstein–Barr virus (EBV), malaria and infectious mononucleosis render the spleen susceptible to spontaneous rupture, but splenectomy will not alter the underlying disease as the question implies.

In agranulocytosis, white blood cells are deficient and hence splenectomy would be detrimental.

1.13 Neck lump   Answers: A B C

Dermoid cysts may arise from epithelium along lines of embryological development. They may arise in the midline of the head and neck and may contain hair or other ectodermal structures.

Sebaceous cysts are the most common skin cysts; they consist of stratified squamous lining epithelium filled with keratin. They are covered by normal epithelium and often have a punctum. They can occur anywhere but tend to occur where hair follicles are present.

A thyroglossal cyst occurs in the midline. It is situated anywhere along the midline usually beneath the hyoid bone along the thyroglossal tract. This is the embryological tract of descent of the thyroid gland from the foramen caecum to its position in the neck. A diagnostic feature is that it moves on swallowing or protrusion of the tongue.

A branchial cyst arises from the remnants of the second pharyngeal pouch. It is typically a painless soft swelling appearing deep to sternomastoid muscle and bulging forward at the anterior border.

Cystic fibromas are lymphangiomas. They are present at birth and may be huge. They occur below the angle of the mandible on the side and not in the midline.

1.14 Carcinoma of the breast   **Answers: A B C D E**
Carcinoma of the breast may present with local symptoms, for example, a lump, nipple discharge/inversion or skin changes, such as lymphoedema.

Paget's disease produces an eczematous change around the nipple. Locally advanced tumours may cause skin ulceration or even necrosis.

Axillary or supraclavicular lymphadenopathy may be presenting features.

Lymphoedema of the arm may be caused by:
- surgery for breast cancer
- radiotherapy to the axilla for breast cancer
- axillary node disease.

Distant spread may occur to the:
- bone (sclerotic as well as lytic lesions)
- liver
- lungs (discrete metastases or lymphangitis)
- brain.

Bone metastases cause fractures as a presenting symptom.

Any lump in the breast is a cancer until or unless proved otherwise. However, benign breast lumps are more common.

1.15 Intravenous urogram   Answers: A B C

A ureteric calculus may cause obstruction to urine flow. The urinary tract proximal to the obstruction therefore becomes dilated and swollen. This is visualized on an intravenous urogram (IVU). For this procedure a 'control' abdominal film (KUB = kidney, ureter and bladder) is taken to look for opacities. Then intravenous contrast medium is injected and further film(s) obtained. Information is obtained about:

- renal size and shape
- speed of excretion of contrast
- ureters

- filling defects / site of obstruction
- bladder.

In acute obstruction the affected kidney is enlarged, whereas the unaffected one is normal in size and function.

1.16 Urinary catheters   Answer: A

A urinary catheter must always be inserted using aseptic techniques to prevent the introduction of infection. Usually a size 14 or 16 Fr catheter is appropriate for catheterization of the male urethra. The size (x3) indicates the external circumference in mm.

Advice should be sought if there has been recent prostate surgery, there is urethral stricture, or the patient has a history of difficult catheterization.

1.17 Renal carcinoma   Answers: B C D

Renal carcinoma is more common in men than in women; the incidence increases after the age of 40. It is an adenocarcinoma and is also known as a hypernephroma because of its resemblance, under the microscope, to adrenal tissue.

Presenting features include:

- haematuria which is usually painless and may be macroscopic or microscopic
- loin pain
- abdominal mass
- pyrexia of unknown origin
- hypertension from excess renin
- polycythaemia from excess erythropoietin

- hypercalcaemia
- secondaries, for example, cannon ball metastases in the lung on chest X-ray or bone metastases
- a left-sided varicocele – this is because the left testicular vein drains into the left renal vein, whereas the right testicular vein drains directly into the inferior vena cava; an obstruction to venous drainage by a left-sided tumour will cause back pressure and hence varicosities of the left testicular vein producing a left-sided varicocele.

1.18 Chest injury   **Answer: None correct**

In any case of trauma the primary survey consists of assessment of:

- Airway
- Breathing
- Circulation

It is important to remember protection of the cervical spine. The patient must be resuscitated to achieve stability of all the above. Following this, a secondary survey must be carried out to assess the patient from head to toe. This may be tailored to more specific areas suggested by the history and examination. The presenting features of a tension pneumothorax are severe shortness of breath and shock. The classical signs of a right-sided pneumothorax include decreased chest wall movement, tracheal deviation to the left, hyper-resonance on the right with absent breath sounds. This is an emergency and requires immediate insertion of a cannula into the second intercostal space on the affected side. Following this a chest X-ray may be obtained.

NB: You should not request a chest X-ray to diagnose a tension pneumothorax!

1.19 Burns   Answers: B C D

The estimation of the area of a burn is done by use of the 'Rule of Nines':

* head   9%
* arm   9% each
* back   18%
* front   18%
* leg   18% each
* palm   1%.

Major burns cause extensive fluid loss and this requires replacement with intravenous colloid and crystalloid. Hypovolaemia, together with haemoconcentration predisposes to thrombosis. The insult to the body causes a stress response and peptic ulceration may result. Another consequence of a major burn is hypothermia, and ice would worsen this.

1.20 Varicose veins   Answers: A E

Varicose veins are dilated superficial veins of the legs. They are due to incompetence of the valves between the superficial and deep systems of venous drainage. The long saphenous system is involved in 90% of cases and the short saphenous system in 10%. Previous deep vein thrombosis predisposes to superficial vein congestion. Varicose veins are a disease of developed countries. Injection sclerotherapy is only of use in minor varicose veins.

Complications include pain (dull ache), cramps, ankle oedema, haemorrhage, thrombophlebitis, lipodermatosclerosis and ulceration.

1.21 Intermittent claudication **Answers: A C D**

Intermittent claudication is characteristically described as pain in the lower limbs which occurs on exercise and is relieved by rest. The pain often occurs in the calf, but can also occur in the thigh or buttock. It is due to atherosclerosis. The outcome varies:

- one-third undergo spontaneous remission
- one-third tolerate symptoms
- one-third experience significant disability and restriction in their daily lives.

These patients go on to develop 'rest pain' and often hang their feet over the side of the bed to ease the pain (increase the blood flow). If left untreated, they may develop necrosis or gangrene and require amputation. Some patients are able to 'walk through their pain'. This encourages the formation of collateral circulation and may help the symptoms.

1.22 Pancreatitis **Answers: A B C D E**

Acute pancreatitis presents as an acute abdomen, with pain in the epigastrium or upper abdomen radiating to the back. It is worsened by movement and the patient can find no relief.

Vomiting is common.

Activated pancreatic enzymes are released into the pancreas, causing inflammation.

Hypocalcaemia develops if there is extensive fat necrosis as calcium is then sequestered. This may produce tetany. A paralytic ileus develops and bowel sounds are often absent. Inflammation of the pancreas with oedema (or a mass in the head of the pancreas) may result in obstruction to the flow of bile and thus cause jaundice.

1.23 Malignant melanoma   Answers: A C D E

A change in the characteristics of a mole may be an indication of malignancy. Changes include:

- surface characteristics, e.g. increase in size, shape or thickness
- change in colour, e.g. darkening in patches
- itching
- bleeding
- brown halo appearance around the lesion
- satellite lesions – these are due to lateral spread around the lesion.

1.24 Fistula   C D E

A fistula is an abnormal connection between two epithelial surfaces. It is lined with granulation tissue but can become epithelialized. The fistula persists if the contents continue to flow along the tract, i.e. if there is distal obstruction to the normal outflow of the contents. If a fistula occurs between two loops of bowel (e.g. small bowel and colon) large amounts of fluid may be lost. A fistula in the anal canal is also known as a fistula *in ano*. It connects the lumen of the anal canal with skin. Anal fistulae are classified into two main groups:

1. Low – below the ano-rectal ring; this type is amenable to surgery by 'laying open' of the fistula which then heals by secondary intention.
2. High – above the ano-rectal ring; this is extremely difficult to treat because surgery may render the patient incontinent.

In contrast, a sinus is a blind ending tract which connects the cavity with an epithelial surface.

1.25 Normal saline   Answers: C D

Normal saline is a solution containing 0.9% NaCl in water. This means there is 0.9 g of NaCl per 100 ml of water. Normal saline contains 154 mmol of sodium per litre; no potassium chloride is added. This concentration makes it isotonic with plasma.

A one molar solution of NaCl would contain 58.5 g (1 mole) of NaCl. In cases of hypovolaemia, intravenous colloid may be given as well as crystalloid to replace electrolytes.

1.26 Metabolic alkalosis   Answers: B D E

Patients with chronic vomiting tend to lose:

- large volumes of water
- HCl (gastric acid in the stomach)
- NaCl/K.

This results in metabolic alkalosis with a rise in pH. It is also known as hypochloraemic alkalosis. Continuous nasal gastric aspiration has the same effect. The patient becomes dehydrated and sodium is depleted. In the compensatory mechanism, the kidney acts to conserve Na^+ in exchange for K^+ and H^+. This is paradoxical aciduria because:

- H^+ is being lost despite the presence of an alkalosis
- hypokalaemia occurs because K^+ is lost in the vomit
- K^+ is lost in the urine
- alkalosis causes K^+ to enter the cells.

1.27 Wound healing   **Answers: A E**
Wound healing depends on:

- a good blood supply
- good apposition of tissues
- tension-free edges.

It is enhanced by a good nutritional state.
The detrimental factors are:

- infection – local or distant – bacterial proteolytic enzymes break down healing tissues
- foreign body, e.g. suture material
- devitalized tissue – due to poor blood supply
- haematoma – prevents good blood supply at the wound edges
- tension
- malnutrition – especially zinc and vitamin C deficiency
- trauma
- metabolic diseases, e.g. diabetes mellitus
- drugs, e.g. cytotoxics and steroids

1.28 Hypovolaemia   **Answers: A C D E**
Hypotension is a sign of 'shock'. A common cause of this is hypovolaemia, e.g. as occurs in a gastrointestinal bleed.

Shock is due to underperfusion of tissues. It is often seen in infarction of the small bowel. Myocardial infarction affects the heart and its function. It may result in a significant decrease in cardiac output; hypoperfusion results and blood pressure falls.

Gram-negative organisms, for example *E. coli*, are well known for producing exotoxins. These act on the circulation and cause vasodilatation which results in hypotension. Intracranial bleeding causes an increase in the intracranial pressure. The effect of this is to decrease heart rate and increase blood pressure (in contrast to hypovolaemia where the cardiovascular response is to increase heart rate and reduce blood pressure).

1.29 Nutritional problems post-gastrectomy

Answers:A C D E

As with any operation, post-operative complications should be considered under the headings 'early', 'intermediate' and 'late', with regard for the general and more specific complications of any particular operation.

Nutritional problems after a gastrectomy take several months to develop. They include:

- Dumping syndrome:
  (a) as food passes rapidly through to the small bowel, the osmotic gradient draws water into the lumen. Hypovolaemia occurs and blood pressure falls; the patient becomes pale, cold and clammy;
  (b) as carbohydrate-rich foods enter the small bowel rapidly, insulin secretion increases. When no further carbohydrate is present a rebound hypoglycaemia results.
- Diarrhoea – this is due to 'blind loop syndrome'. In the Polya type gastrectomy a blind ending loop of duodenum harbours bacteria. Bacterial overgrowth then results in diarrhoea and malabsorption. Diarrhoea may be severe and episodic.
- Vomiting – due to overfilling of the stomach. Sometimes bilious vomiting occurs before a meal as bile refluxes into the stomach remnant.

- Weight loss – due to vomiting/diarrhoea and poor appetite (as there is no stomach there is no reservoir).
- Vitamin B12 deficiency – loss of gastric intrinsic factor results in malabsorption of vitamin B12. This causes a macrocytic megaloblastic anaemia. It takes between about three months to several years to develop as body stores are used up.
- Iron deficiency anaemia – normally the acid pH of the stomach increases iron absorption in the Fe^{3+} state. Therefore reduced iron absorption results in iron deficiency anaemia.
- Osteomalacia – this is due to malabsorption of calcium and vitamin D. Also the acid pH of the stomach reduces calcium absorption.
- Steatorrhoea – this is due to poor mixing of food and enzymes, reduced pancreatic output and inactivation of enzymes in the afferent loops.

Other complications are:

- a feeling of fullness (the patient needs to eat small amounts of food frequently)
- gastric outlet obstruction
- ulceration in the gastric remnant (rare)
- tumour in the gastric remnant.

1.30 Subphrenic abscess   Answers: B C D

A subphrenic abscess occurs as a complication of intra-abdominal infection or surgery. The patient typically develops abdominal pain and a swinging pyrexia with sepsis where no other cause (e.g. chest or bladder infection) can be found. *E. coli* and Bacteroides are the most common offending organisms.

A subphrenic abscess can occur on the left or right side of the abdomen.

On the right side it occurs between the diaphragm and the liver. It communicates with the peritoneal cavity. Infection here commonly arises from the gallbladder or small bowel perforation.

Infection from the right kidney may also result in a right-sided subphrenic abscess.

On the left side it occurs between the diaphragm and left lobe of the liver with the spleen further to the left. Infection is associated with gastric perforation or from colon, pancreas or spleen.

Diaphragmatic irritation causes hiccoughs.

Investigations show:

- ESR – raised
- white cell count – raised
- CXR – pleural effusion occurs on the side of the abscess
- empyema may occur
- ultrasound scan and CT scan – collections are visualized.

The treatment is:

- conservative with antibiotics
- drainage – this is the more definitive treatment; it can be by ultrasound or CT-guided.

Alternatively, surgery may be required.

1.31 Horner's syndrome   Answers: B C E

The features of Horner's syndrome are ptosis, miosis, anhydrosis and enophthalmos. Horner's syndrome is due to damage of the sympathetic nerves to the head and neck. The nerves involved are from T1 and its post-ganglionic connections, which synapse in the cervical ganglia. Interruption of the sympathetic nerve supply causes:

- the pupil to constrict
- blood vessels to dilate – vasoconstriction
- reduced sweating
- drooping of *levator palpebrae superioris*; this muscle of the eyelid is supplied by sympathetic nerves as well as cranial nerve 3. Interruption of sympathetic nerve function results in partial ptosis.

The causes of Horner's syndrome are:

- brachial plexus injury
- cervical sympathectomy – iatrogenic
- lung tumours, i.e. pancoast tumour in the apex of the lung
- brain lesions
- syringomyelia or spinal cord lesions
- carotid artery aneurysm
- tumours in the neck.

1.32 Acute appendicitis   Answers: A B E

Acute appendicitis is a very common surgical emergency. The classical symptoms are as follows:

- pain – this starts as central abdominal pain which shifts to the right iliac fossa
- anorexia (before pain)

- nausea and vomiting
- constipation, but diarrhoea may occur.

The typical signs are:

- the patient is pale and flushed, especially in children the tongue is furred with *fetor oris*
- there is rebound tenderness and guarding in the right iliac fossa
- pyrexia (but the patient may be apyrexial) – if the temperature is greater than 38°C consider perforation
- rectal examination may reveal tenderness in the right pelvic area.

The appendix is a vestigial organ attached to the caecum. Usually infection develops in the appendix because it is obstructed by a faecalith.

1.33 Bell's palsy   **Answers: A B**

Bell's palsy is a lower motor neurone lesion of the 7th cranial nerve, i.e. the facial nerve. The facial nerve supplies the muscles of the facial expression, sensation to the external auditory meatus, salivary and lacrimal glands, and has a branch to stapedius. The features are:

- loss of facial expression on the affected side; there is drooping of the lip and lower eyelid. The patient is unable to smile, whistle or frown. On attempted closure of the eye, the eye tends to roll upwards. The lower eyelid droops and hence complete eye closure is not possible. The patient may require a protective eye patch and hypromellose eye drops to keep the eyes moist
- loss of lacrimation
- loss of taste in the anterior two-thirds of the tongue

- there may be pain around the ear, due to inflammation
- hyperacusis occurs if the nerve to stapedius is affected.

With a lower motor neurone lesion the entire side of the face is paralysed. In an upper motor neurone lesion the upper facial muscles are not affected because occipitofrontalis has a bilateral innervation. Hence when the patient is asked to raise the eyebrows, he is still able to do so.

The cause of a Bell's palsy is unknown, although there may be a history of a previous viral illness. Treatment is conservative; the symptoms resolve with time. Steroids may be given, but their use is controversial. Forty per cent of patients do not fully recover. A 7th nerve lesion associated with *Herpes zoster* virus causing lesions in the external auditory meatus is known as the Ramsay Hunt syndrome.

1.34 Medial meniscal tear   Answers: A B C D E

Medial meniscal tears occur more frequently than lateral tears because the medial meniscus is attached to the capsule of the knee joint. This makes it less mobile and trauma results in a tear.

If the cartilage then becomes jammed between the articular surfaces of the tibia and femur, 'locking' of the knee is felt, where full extension of the knee is not possible. Full flexion is still possible.

The patient may complain that the knee 'gives way'. The history is usually of a twisting injury resulting in pain and swelling due to recurrent effusions which may be haemarthrosis. In long-standing cases, quadriceps wasting occurs. Investigations include arthroscopy or MRI.

Treatment:

- conservative – the leg is put in plaster with the knee extended for 3–4 weeks
- operative – this can be done at arthroscopy, for example, suturing or partial meniscectomy

1.35 Avascular necrosis   Answers: A B C D E

Avascular necrosis is ischaemic necrosis of bone. It is caused by interruption of the blood supply to the bone. It is a well known complication of:

- trauma, such as
    fractures, e.g. of the scaphoid, femoral neck, (subcapital), humeral head, lunate and talus
    dislocation, e.g. lunate bone
    caissons disease
- infection, e.g. tuberculosis
- neoplastic lesions
- metabolic, e.g. Gaucher's disease
- connective tissue disease
- drugs, e.g. high dose steroids
- alcohol abuse
- vascular disease, e.g. sickle cell disease
- idiopathic, e.g. Perthe's disease.

There is a useful mnemonic for remembering the causes of any condition: *TIN MAN CAN DRIVE*

Trauma
Infection
Neoplasia

Metabolic
Autoimmune
Nutritional
Connective tissue
Ageing
Neurological
Drugs
Radiotherapy
Idiopathic
Vascular
Endocrine.

1.36 Neuromuscular blockers   Answer: E

Muscle relaxants are often used during surgery.
Neuromuscular blockers are of two types:

- Competitive inhibitors (e.g. tubocurarine, pancuronium, atracuronium and vecuronium). The agents are reversible; they act by competing with acetylcholine for the receptor site. Remember that the neurotransmitter at the neuromuscular junction is acetylcholine acting on muscarinic receptors. Increasing concentration of tubocurarine, for example, displaces acetylcholine and vice versa. Their action is terminated by use of an anticholinesterase (e.g. neostigmine).
- Depolarizing blockers (e.g. suxamethonium); this is irreversible, the initial action is to cause stimulation and hence muscle fasciculation may be seen. Patients often complain of muscular pain following an operation where suxamethonium has been administered. Suxamethonium has a rapid onset and is short acting. It is normally metabolized by pseudocholinesterase. Note that some patients have a deficiency of this enzyme and in these cases the effects may be devas-

tating. The deficiency is often familial and therefore a family history is very important.

1.37 Carcinoma of the stomach **Answers: B C D E**
Carcinoma of the stomach is usually adenocarcinoma. The aetiology is unknown. The associations include:

- genetics – first-degree relatives have an increased incidence
- blood group A (whereas duodenal ulcers occur more in blood group O)
- geographical (for example, the incidence is higher in Japan; this is probably an environmental effect)
- social class – the incidence is higher in the lower social classes
- gastric mucosal atrophy predisposes to carcinoma (for example, gastritis and pernicious anaemia)
- polycyclic hydrocarbons and nitrosamines in the diet have been implicated
- cigarette smoking.

Carcinoma of the stomach is rare before the age of 50 years; it is more common in males than in females. Spread occurs locally, via the bloodstream and via the lymphatic system. Transcoelomic spread to the ovaries results in 'Krukenberg tumours'.

1.38 Minimally invasive surgery **Answers: A B C**
Minimally invasive surgery refers to those procedures which are performed with minimal access, for example, laparoscopic surgery or ultrasound-guided abscess drainage. The incision is kept small. Laparoscopic surgery is used commonly for cholecystectomy and hernia repair

(keyhole surgery) but is also used for appendicectomy, fundoplication, hemicolectomy, sympathectomy and nephrectomy. The advantages are:

- less operative trauma
- a reduction in post-operative complications
- quicker recovery time and mobility.

The disadvantages are:

- it takes longer (especially for inexperienced surgeons)
- it is costly
- exposure is limited
- it has its own risks (for example, bowel injury during introduction of the Veres needle or increased risk of bile duct injury during laparoscopic cholecystectomy.

1.39 Sarcoma   **Answers: A B C D**

Sarcoma is a Greek word meaning 'fleshy growth'. It refers to a malignant tumour arising in the tissues of mesenchymal origin, for example, skeletal tissues. The suffix 'sarcoma' is used to denote malignancy, for example, in bone it is osteosarcoma, in smooth muscle it is leiomyosarcoma. Osteosarcoma occurs most commonly in the metaphyses of the femur. The cause is mostly unknown. However, there are several associations:

- inherited conditions (e.g. neurofibromatosis)
- ionizing radiation
- scars from thermal and acid burns
- Kaposi's sarcoma, seen in AIDS.

Sarcomas tend to grow rapidly. Spread, as with any tumour, is:
- local
- via the blood stream (this is the predominant route of spread)
- via lymphatics.

Note that in tumours such as those of the stomach, spread may occur via peritoneal fluids, i.e. transcoelomic spread.

Treatment of sarcomas is by a combination of surgery and radiotherapy. Adjuvant chemotherapy is controversial.

1.40 Prostate carcinoma   Answers: A C D E

Carcinoma of the prostate is the commonest malignant condition in males aged over 65 years. A patient typically presents with:
- no symptoms
- bladder outflow obstruction, i.e. hesitancy, poor stream, frequency, nocturia, post-micturition dribbling
- manifestations of spread (see below).

The modes of spread are:
- Local spread – this involves local tissue especially the rectum and may cause a stricture; the patient complains of change in bowel habit. Local spread may cause a major deep vein thrombosis of the lower limbs by obstructing venous return.
- Distance spread – via the blood stream, especially to the pelvis and vertebrae; lesions are typically sclerotic. Patients present with bone pain or pathological fractures. The rate of growth depends on testosterone concentration.

Treatment:

- hormonal manipulation:
  orchidectomy
  oestrogen
  luteinizing hormone releasing hormone
  anti-androgens, such as cyproterone acetate (CPA).
- for early tumours – transurethral resection of the prostate
- radiotherapy.

When determining the pathology of a condition use the mnemonic:

*In **A** Surgeon's **G**own **A** Physician **M**ay **M**ake **S**ome **T**erribly **C**lever **P**rogress*

Incidence
Age
Sex
Geography
Aetiology
Predisposition
Macroscopic features
Microscopic features
Spread
Treatment
Complications
Prognosis

1.41 Post-operative complications   Answers: C D E
Post-operative complications are best organized under the headings 'Early', 'Intermediate' and 'Late':

- Early – up to 24 hours
  atelectasis/respiratory distress
  reactionary haemorrhage
- Intermediate – second day to two weeks
  lungs – atelectasis, infection, pulmonary embolism
  bladder – urinary retention, urinary tract infection
  legs – deep vein thrombosis
  wound infection, dehiscence
- Late – weeks later
  wound dehiscence
  incisional hernia
  recurrent condition.

These are general complications. Further consideration needs to be given to the complications associated with specific operations, for example, anastomotic leak in bowel surgery or nutritional complications following gastrectomy, paralytic ileus and subphrenic abscesses following abdominal surgery.

1.42 Gas gangrene   Answers: B C

Gas gangrene develops when there is wound infection with *Clostridium perfringens*, a Gram-positive rod found in soil. It is an obligate anaerobe and therefore proliferates under anaerobic conditions. The organisms produce exotoxins which destroy tissue and result in necrosis. It produces gases which can be felt as 'crepitus'. Tissue destruction is rapid, initially blackening the skin which breaks down and becomes purulent. Necrosis occurs.

Treatment is:

- excision of necrotic tissue – the wound should be left open to allow drainage and NOT sutured; dressing

packs are used to facilitate healing from inside out
- intravenous benzylpenicillin – should be given prophylactically in injury or before amputation of a limb
- hyperbaric oxygen therapy
- antitoxin administration.

1.43 Fibroadenosis   A E

Fibroadenosis is a benign disorder of the breast where there is an abnormal response of tissue growth to the hormonal cycle. It may represent the extreme end of a normal range. It is not pre-cancerous but cancer may coexist and hence be misdiagnosed. Fibroadenosis (also called fibrocystic disease or painful nodularity) presents with:

- one or more multiple lumps
- cysts
- diffuse nodularity
- pain or tenderness.

These changes tend to occur in a cyclical fashion. The treatment is:

- reassure
- lumpectomy
- mastectomy – very rare and only in severe debilitating cases.

1.44 Gynaecomastia   Answers: B E

Gynaecomastia is a benign condition where there is enlargement of the male breast.

The causes are:

- physiological – neonatal or pubertal
- idiopathic – this is the most common non-physiological cause; it may be unilateral or bilateral
- chronic liver disease, e.g. alcoholism, cirrhosis
- hormones, for example, oestrogens; in testicular atrophy hormonal abnormality may occur; hormone producing tumours
- drugs, such as oestrogens – stilboestrol (given in prostatic carcinoma), spironolactone, digoxin, cimetidine, steroids.

1.45 Abdominal aortic aneurysm   Answers: A C
An aneurysm is a localized dilatation of an artery involving all the layers of the wall. It may be fusiform or saccular. The most common cause is atherosclerosis. Other causes include:

- congenital aneurysms
- trauma
- syphilis
- collagen diseases (e.g. Marfan's syndrome or Ehlers–Danlos syndrome).

A genetic disposition has been found. The incidence is higher in males aged over 60 years; it is associated with hypertension and smoking.

It may be asymptomatic or produce a pulsatile mass in the abdomen, with abdominal pain radiating to the back, and 'shock' if a leak or rupture occurs.

Aneurysms are most frequently found in the abdominal aorta and below. They are usually below the renal arteries. Calcification along the arterial wall often allows visualization on a plain abdominal film. Other useful investigations are ultrasound scan, CT scan and aortography which are used to assess size.

Size is monitored with serial ultrasound scans; elective surgery is indicated when the aortic diameter is greater than 5 cm, although this limit varies, depending on the fitness of the patient for surgery and the rate of expansion of the aneurysm. The risk of rupture increases with size and when symptoms occur. Surgery involves repair of the aneurysm with a prosthetic graft.

1.46 Nasogastric tube (NGT)   **Answers: C E**

In severe head injury where there is loss of the gag reflex, the airway needs to be protected. This can be done with a cuffed endotracheal tube. Insertion of a nasogastric tube is contraindicated in basal skull fractures as there is a risk of pushing the tube into the brain.

In small or large bowel obstruction the first line of treatment is 'drip and suck', i.e. intravenous fluid maintenance and suction of stomach contents via a nasogastric tube. The NGT is put on free drainage with aspiration at regular intervals. This relieves vomiting, protects the airway, and protects the dilated bowel from any further fluid and air. These conservative measures may be enough to relieve the obstruction. If not, surgery is required. Nasogastric aspiration is not useful in assessing upper gastrointestinal blood loss as a considerable amount of blood may be lost into the lumen and appear as melaena. A fine bore NGT is used for enteral feeding.

1.47 Pleomorphic adenoma (mixed parotid tumour)
Answers:A D E

Pleomorphic adenoma is an adenoma of salivary glands. Typically it presents as a painless slow-growing mass in the parotid gland. It is a benign tumour. The capsule is incomplete and the tumour may penetrate into surrounding tissue. It may then recur or undergo malignant transformation. Thus, enucleation is not enough for removal – excision is required.

At surgery, there is a risk of facial nerve damage as the facial nerve branches within the gland. Frey's syndrome occurs when the parasympathetic secretomotor nerve fibres to the gland are divided and then regenerate in the skin. This causes sweating on stimulation of the salivary gland, i.e. 'gustatory sweating'.

1.48 Paralytic ileus   A B D
Causes of paralytic ileus are as follows:

- laparotomy, i.e. handling of the bowel prolongs the ileus
- hypokalaemia
- peritonitis
- renal failure
- trauma (e.g. fracture of a lumbar vertebra)

Calcium is not implicated. Lumbar sympathectomy seems to prevent paralytic ileus.

1.49 Carcinoma of the oesophagus   Answers: A B D E
Most carcinomas of the oesophagus are squamous cell tumours occurring in the middle third of the oesophagus.

The risk factors are alcohol, smoking and diet (nitrosamines).

There is an association with structural abnormalities, for example, achalasia, oesophageal webs, strictures, pharyngeal pouch and Barrett's oesophagus.

Plummer–Vinson syndrome consists of dysphagia due to an oesophageal web with iron deficiency anaemia and is associated with carcinoma of the oesophagus.

1.50 Acute cholecystitis – treatment   **Answers:A B C D**
Uncomplicated acute cholecystitis will resolve with conservative treatment, i.e. bed rest, intravenous fluids, intravenous antibiotics and analgesia. Cholecystectomy may be performed early or late – about six weeks after the acute attack has settled. Laparoscopic or open technique may be used.

50 questions: time allowed 2 hours.
Mark your answers with a tick (True) or a cross (False) in
the box provided. Leave the box blank for 'Don't know'.
Do not look at the answers until you have completed the
whole question paper.

2.1 The following occur in gastro-oesophageal reflux:

- ☐ A pneumonia
- ☐ B oesophageal stricture
- ☐ C iron deficiency anaemia
- ☐ D polyneuritis
- ☐ E pernicious anaemia

2.2 In gastric ulceration

- ☐ A malignant change eventually supervenes
- ☐ B an hour-glass stomach may occur
- ☐ C excess acid secretion is the main cause
- ☐ D carbenoxolone sodium may promote healing
- ☐ E the majority of benign ulcers are situated in the greater curvature

2.3 Familial adenomatous polyposis

- ☐ A may be inherited as an autosomal dominant condition
- ☐ B is pre-malignant
- ☐ C occurs in severe ulcerative colitis
- ☐ D may cause electrolyte disturbance
- ☐ E may be asymptomatic

2.4 Crohn's disease

- ☐ A is familial
- ☐ B is malignant
- ☐ C Reed–Sternberg cells are pathognomonic
- ☐ D produces caseating granulomas
- ☐ E is a transmural disease of the small bowel only

2.5 Symptoms of mesenteric embolus include

- ☐ A rebound tenderness
- ☐ B melaena
- ☐ C hypotension
- ☐ D visible peristalsis
- ☐ E haematemesis

2.6 Constipation may be due to

- ☐ A opiates
- ☐ B aluminium hydroxide preparations
- ☐ C hypothyroidism
- ☐ D diabetes mellitus
- ☐ E lactulose

2.7 Regarding haemorrhoids

- [ ] A thrombosis is a recognized complication
- [ ] B they can be treated with band ligation
- [ ] C first-degree piles are best treated with haemorrhoidectomy
- [ ] D they predispose to carcinoma
- [ ] E strangulation can be treated with haemorrhoidectomy

2.8 Symptoms of a strangulated femoral hernia include

- [ ] A irreducibility
- [ ] B overlying redness
- [ ] C tenderness
- [ ] D diarrhoea
- [ ] E a fluid thrill on coughing

2.9 Investigation of Crohn's disease often reveals

- [ ] A a lead-pipe colon on barium enema
- [ ] B increased uptake on a white cell scan
- [ ] C rose thorn ulcers
- [ ] D strictures
- [ ] E toxic megacolon

2.10 Recognized modes of presentation of gallstones include

- ☐ A dysphagia
- ☐ B abdominal pain
- ☐ C a symptomless mass in the right upper quadrant
- ☐ D small bowel obstruction
- ☐ E tenesmus

2.11 Common signs of obstructive jaundice are

- ☐ A dark stools
- ☐ B dark urine
- ☐ C splenomegaly
- ☐ D itching
- ☐ E a palpable gallbladder

2.12 Features of hydatid cysts in the liver include

- ☐ A menorrhagia
- ☐ B calcification on a plain abdominal X-ray
- ☐ C haemoptysis
- ☐ D anaphylaxis
- ☐ E jaundice

2.13 A swelling presenting just below the angle of the mandible in a 30-year-old male may be

- ☐ A a pharyngeal pouch
- ☐ B an enlarged lymph node
- ☐ C a thyroglossal cyst
- ☐ D a carotid body tumour
- ☐ E ectopic thyroid tissue

2.14 Incidence of carcinoma of the breast increases if

- ☐ A the contralateral breast is affected
- ☐ B the patient is young
- ☐ C the patient has breast-fed
- ☐ D the patient is obese
- ☐ E a first-degree relative had it

2.15 A hydrocoele

- ☐ A may be pre-malignant
- ☐ B may occur after repair of a hernia
- ☐ C occurs in the *processus vaginalis*
- ☐ D causes infertility
- ☐ E is reducible

2.16 A patient presents with a large swelling confined to the scrotum. It is transilluminable and the testis can be felt separately. The diagnosis may be

- ☐ A a hydrocoele
- ☐ B an inguinal hernia
- ☐ C hydrocoele of the cord
- ☐ D an epididymal cyst
- ☐ E epididymal tuberculosis

2.17 Acute renal failure following major abdominal surgery may be caused by

- ☐ A hypotension during operation
- ☐ B a haemolytic transfusion reaction
- ☐ C Gram-negative septicaemia
- ☐ D a renal calculus
- ☐ E deep vein thrombosis

2.18 After a head injury an extradural haematoma

- ☐ A can be confidently excluded if the patient is conscious
- ☐ B causes dilatation of the contralateral pupil at an early stage
- ☐ C causes a deterioration in the levels of consciousness
- ☐ D is always associated with a fractured skull
- ☐ E is characteristically associated with an increased heart rate and blood pressure

2.19 An undescended testis

☐ A should be brought into the scrotum after the age of 10 years
☐ B is rarely associated with an inguinal hernia
☐ C is prone to malignant change
☐ D is more likely to undergo torsion than a normal testis
☐ E means that the patient will be sterile

2.20 A varicocele

☐ A may be treated by sclerotherapy
☐ B is usually right-sided
☐ C is associated with renal tumour
☐ D can be treated by embolization
☐ E may cause pain

2.21 Raynaud's phenomenon may be secondary to

☐ A carcinoma of the oesophagus
☐ B pernicious anaemia
☐ C atheroma of the subclavian artery
☐ D carcinoma of the testis
☐ E rheumatoid arthritis

2.22 Complications of acute pancreatitis include

- ☐ A carcinoma of the pancreas
- ☐ B stones in the common bile duct
- ☐ C pseudocyst formation
- ☐ D obstruction of the transverse colon
- ☐ E fat embolus

2.23 Rodent ulcers

- ☐ A are squamous cell carcinomas
- ☐ B are basal cell carcinomas
- ☐ C only occur on the face
- ☐ D show epithelial pearls
- ☐ E metastasize to the blood stream

2.24 Recurrent anal fistulae are associated with

- ☐ A Crohn's disease
- ☐ B ulcerative colitis
- ☐ C carcinoma
- ☐ D Peutz–Jeghers syndrome
- ☐ E diverticular disease

2.25 A patient aged 65 years presents with severe abdominal pain radiating to the back, abdominal distension and hypotension. The likely diagnosis is

☐ A a leaking aortic aneurysm
☐ B renal colic
☐ C acute appendicitis
☐ D acute pancreatitis
☐ E pelvic inflammatory disease

2.26 Tetany is a recognized complication of

☐ A metabolic alkalosis
☐ B thyroidectomy
☐ C a deep dirty wound of the foot
☐ D over-breathing
☐ E paralytic ileus

2.27 An acutely infected ingrowing toe nail may be treated by

☐ A Keller's osteotomy
☐ B amputation of the toe
☐ C lateral wedge excision of the nail and nail bed
☐ D antibiotics
☐ E nail avulsion

2.28 In a man aged 50 years with a three-year history of indigestion, the management of 1 litre haematemesis should be as follows:

☐ A a barium meal should be performed within 24 hours
☐ B gastroscopy must be postponed for 48 hours after the last episode of bleeding
☐ C in view of the history an operation should follow initial resuscitation
☐ D blood transfusion should be started if the haemoglobin is less than 9 g/dl
☐ E a careful watch should be kept on the pulse, blood pressure and central venous pressure

2.29 A pilonidal sinus is

☐ A a sinus containing hair
☐ B a fistula *in ano* containing hair
☐ C an abscess in a hair-bearing area
☐ D a sinus which commonly occurs in the natal cleft
☐ E often associated with a number of subcutaneous tracks

2.30 Malignant melanoma

☐ A are not always pigmented
☐ B may arise from junctional naevi
☐ C may itch
☐ D metastases in regional lymph nodes are very effectively treated by external radiotherapy
☐ E regress after hypophysectomy

2.31 Buerger's disease or *thrombophlebitis obliterans*

☐ A affects young men
☐ B is confined to smokers
☐ C involves upper limb and lower limb arteries
☐ D is usually associated with Raynaud's phenomenon
☐ E affects the veins as well as the arteries

2.32 Carotid artery stenosis

☐ A may be asymptomatic
☐ B causes *amaurosis fugax*
☐ C causes vomiting
☐ D causes transient ischaemic attacks
☐ E is treated with carotid endarterectomy if the stenosis is 20%

2.33 In anal fissures the treatment is

☐ A laxatives
☐ B anal dilatation
☐ C examination under anaesthetic
☐ D often not required
☐ E excision of the fissure

2.34 Carpal tunnel syndrome may result in

☐   A   hypothenar wasting
☐   B   wasting of the interossei
☐   C   reduced sensation over the index finger
☐   D   a positive Tinel's sign
☐   E   pain in the forearm

2.35 In a compound fracture

☐   A   by definition the bone is broken into many fragments
☐   B   the overlying soft tissues are broken with free communication to the exterior
☐   C   patients should be given appropriate antibiotic cover
☐   D   operative fixation of the fracture is contraindicated
☐   E   the bone is by definition broken in two or more places

2.36 Ranitidine

☐   A   acts by blocking histamine receptors
☐   B   is an H_1 antagonist
☐   C   is used to prevent stress ulcers
☐   D   can be given intravenously
☐   E   should be avoided in the first 12 hours following a gastrointestinal bleed

2.37 A peptic ulcer

☐ A only occurs in the stomach
☐ B may give rise to haemorrhage
☐ C may produce obstruction in the duodenum
☐ D is always associated with stress
☐ E may be associated with hyperparathyroidism

2.38 The following are more likely to occur in ulcerative colitis than in Crohn's disease:

☐ A rectal bleeding
☐ B abdominal mass
☐ C steatorrhoea
☐ D rectal involvement
☐ E fistulae

2.39 Dupuytren's contracture is

☐ A more common in men than in women
☐ B associated with alcoholic cirrhosis of the liver
☐ C associated with underlying malignancy
☐ D transmitted as an autosomal recessive condition
☐ E associated with renal failure

2.40 A closed fracture of the femoral shaft

☐ A may be complicated by fat embolism
☐ B may require blood transfusion
☐ C requires tetanus immunization
☐ D may require intra-medullary nailing
☐ E will have healed fully within six weeks

2.41 Eighteen hours after an operation it is noticed that a patient has not passed urine. Which of the following would always be appropriate:

☐ A intravenous infusion of 10% mannitol
☐ B injection of 20 mg frusemide
☐ C catheterization of the bladder
☐ D examination of the bladder
☐ E renal dose of dopamine

2.42 Cellulitis is a term used to describe

☐ A death of liver cells in association with circulating toxins
☐ B inflammation surrounding a malignant tumour
☐ C spreading infection in the subcutaneous tissue
☐ D tuberculosis involving the skin
☐ E an abscess occurring in a surgical wound

2.43 Meckel's diverticulum

- [ ] A is seen in 20% of the population
- [ ] B is a remnant of the vitello-intestinal duct
- [ ] C is a small appendix
- [ ] D is associated with peptic ulceration
- [ ] E may present as acute appendicitis

2.44 Salivary duct calculi

- [ ] A are more common in the parotid duct than in the submandibular duct
- [ ] B are usually radio-opaque
- [ ] C cause pain on eating
- [ ] D can be confirmed with sialography
- [ ] E are usually treated with surgical removal of the gland

2.45 Cancer of the stomach

- [ ] A has a five-year survival rate of more than 40%
- [ ] B is commonest in the antrum
- [ ] C metastasizes to lymph nodes
- [ ] D may present with an abdominal mass
- [ ] E is treated with gastrectomy

2.46 Ureteric calculi

- ☐ A produce pain that is colicky in nature
- ☐ B should routinely be surgically removed
- ☐ C are predominantly 'triple phosphate'
- ☐ D can be treated by lithotripsy
- ☐ E predispose to transitional cell carcinoma of the ureter

2.47 The normal metabolic response to trauma is characterized by

- ☐ A an increase in lean body mass
- ☐ B antidiuretic hormone release
- ☐ C gluconeogenesis
- ☐ D a positive nitrogen balance
- ☐ E potassium loss

2.48 The passage of bright red blood with faeces may be caused by

- ☐ A thrombosed haemorrhoid
- ☐ B anal fissure
- ☐ C ischiorectal abscess
- ☐ D carcinoma of the colon at the hepatic flexure
- ☐ E haemorrhoids

2.49 Staging of breast tumours

☐ A assesses extent of spread
☐ B indicates prognosis
☐ C does not take account of nodal involvement
☐ D is performed by mammography
☐ E is only of use in females

2.50 Hypocalcaemia may occur in

☐ A multiple myeloma
☐ B parathyroid adenoma
☐ C acute pancreatitis
☐ D gallstones
☐ E post-thyroidectomy

───────────────── **END** ─────────────────

Go over your answers until your time is up.
Correct answers and teaching notes are overleaf.

The correct answer options for each question are given below.

2.1	A B C	2.26	A B D
2.2	B D	2.27	C D E
2.3	A B D E	2.28	D E
2.4	None correct	2.29	A D E
2.5	A B C	2.30	A B C
2.6	A B C	2.31	A B C E
2.7	A B E	2.32	A B D
2.8	A B C	2.33	A B D
2.9	B C	2.34	C D E
2.10	B D	2.35	B C
2.11	B D E	2.36	A C D
2.12	B C D E	2.37	B C E
2.13	B D	2.38	A D
2.14	A D E	2.39	A B
2.15	B C	2.40	A B D
2.16	C D	2.41	C D
2.17	A B C	2.42	C
2.18	C	2.43	B D E
2.19	C D	2.44	B C D
2.20	C D E	2.45	B C D E
2.21	C E	2.46	A D
2.22	C E	2.47	B C E
2.23	B	2.48	B E
2.24	A B C	2.49	A B
2.25	A C D	2.50	C D E

2.1 Hiatus hernia with reflux   Answers: A B C

Reflux of acid from the stomach into the oesophagus causes oesophagitis. This presents with retrosternal pain, regurgitation and dyspepsia. Bleeding may occur resulting in iron deficiency anaemia. In chronic oesophagitis, fibrosis occurs which may result in stricture formation and then present as dysphagia. Metaplasia of oesophageal epithelium from squamous to columnar may occur. This is known as Barrett's oesophagus, which is pre-malignant. Pernicious anaemia is associated with atrophic gastritis, NOT oesophagitis.

Reflux may be so marked that it causes overspill into the trachea. This is particularly marked at night when the patient lies flat causing 'nocturnal asthma'; pneumonitis may occur. Other modes of presentation are halitosis and hoarseness of the voice.

2.2 Gastric ulcers   Answers: B D

Most gastric ulcers occur on the lesser curve. Frequency increases with age and there is an association with blood group A. It is more common in lower socio-economic classes. Acid secretion tends to be normal or low. The main problem is thought to be reduced mucosal resistance to acid (in contrast with duodenal ulcers where acid secretion is abnormally high).

Cigarette smoking is another association.

Helicobacter pylori is associated with both gastric and duodenal ulcers and therefore eradication therapy plays an important role.

Weight loss is a significant symptom in gastric ulceration

as eating often causes pain, whereas in duodenal ulceration pain is relieved by food.

Gastric ulceration may be benign or malignant. Whether benign ulcers progress to malignancy remains controversial.

2.3   Familial adenomatous polyposis   Answers: A B D E
Familial adenomatous polyposis (FAP) is an autosomal dominant inherited condition. It is characterized by multiple polyps throughout the colon and rectum. It develops in teenage years when it is initially asymptomatic and benign. Later, symptoms develop and patients present with a change in bowel habit, i.e. loose stools, rectal bleeding and mucus per rectum. Malignant change inevitably occurs within 20 years. Prophylactic surgery is the treatment of choice with total colectomy and ileorectal anastomosis or pouch-anal anastomosis. In ulcerative colitis, inflammatory polyps may occur, but this is not the inherited condition FAP. Electrolyte disturbance occurs when there is considerable loss of mucus and blood per rectum.

2.4   Crohn's disease   Answer: None correct
The aetiology of Crohn's disease is unknown. There may be a genetic predisposition as there is an association with family history.

Pathology: Crohn's disease can occur anywhere along the gastrointestinal tract from the mouth to the anus. It is characterized by:

● transmural involvement of the bowel, i.e. it affects the whole thickness of the wall

- granuloma formation (non-caseating)
- skip lesions, i.e. patchy involvement with normal areas in between
- inflammation and oedema of the bowel wall
- deep ulceration.

It is NOT a malignant condition.

Reed–Sternberg cells are seen in Hodgkin's disease.

2.5 Mesenteric embolus   Answers: A B C

Mesenteric ischaemia is a lack of blood supply to the mesentery. This may be due to:

- embolus
- thrombosis
- reduced cardiac output (e.g. due to myocardial infarction)
- blocked venous drainage
- hypovolaemia.

In mesenteric embolus, oedema of the bowel wall may result in rupture of blood vessels resulting in haemorrhage into the bowel. The signs are:

- abdominal pain with rebound tenderness
- pyrexia
- dehydration
- vomiting
- white cell count $> 30,000$ /mm^3
- acidosis.

Abdominal signs are often mild and deceptive, even with extensive bowel damage.

The signs of generalized peritonitis occur if there is perforation. Ninety per cent of mesenteric emboli arise from the heart in association with atrial fibrillation. The extent of bowel affected depends on the site of final impaction.

2.6 Constipation   **Answers: A B C**
The causes of constipation are:

- drugs (e.g. opiates, iron, aluminium hydroxide preparations)
- hypothyroidism
- inactivity
- low fibre diet
- faecal impaction
- bowel strictures (e.g. in diverticular disease or carcinoma).

'Absolute constipation' refers to the absence of flatus and faeces.

2.7 Haemorrhoids   **Answers: A B E**
See also the explanation to Paper 1, Question 7.

The management of haemorrhoids is as follows:

- conservative – high fibre diet, avoidance of straining, and good anal hygiene
- medical – local anaesthetic agents, steroids and symptomatic relief
- surgical – submucosal injection, banding, and anal dilatation are used for first and second-degree haemorrhoids; haemorrhoidectomy is used for third or fourth-degree haemorrhoids.

2.8 Femoral hernia   **Answers: A B C**
See also Paper 1, Question 8.

A strangulated femoral hernia typically presents as an irreducible lump in the groin, with pain and tenderness. Overlying redness occurs due to local inflammation especially in obstruction. If there is obstruction then vomiting, abdominal distension and constipation occur. A fluid thrill on coughing suggests a saphena varix.

2.9 Crohn's disease – X-ray features   **Answers: B C**
Crohn's disease is investigated with contrast studies:

- small bowel – a small bowel meal and follow through or small bowel enema
- large bowel – barium enema.

X-rays show:

- terminal ileum irregularity of the mucosa
- rose thorn ulcers
- cobblestone appearance of the mucosa
- narrowing where there is fibrosis producing strictures
- dilatation of the bowel proximal to strictures
- fistulae.

White cell scans are performed to localize sites of inflammation.

Colonoscopy is often helpful to obtain biopsies.

The 'lead-pipe colon' is a feature of ulcerative colitis where there is loss of haustrae.

Toxic megacolon is a feature of ulcerative colitis.

2.10 Gallstones   Answers: B D

The modes of presentation of gallstones are:

- asymptomatic, i.e. incidental finding
- acute cholecystitis – this occurs when a stone in the cystic duct or bile duct causes inflammation and transient obstruction
- chronic cholecystitis
- biliary colic due to attempts to pass the stone
- acute pancreatitis when stones impact in the ampulla of Vater
- obstructive jaundice
- small bowel obstruction due to 'gallstone ileus'; stones may impact in the terminal ileum
- empyema – a pus-filled gallbladder following stone impaction causes a swinging pyrexia and systemic illness
- perforation of the gallbladder producing peritonitis.

2.11 Obstructive jaundice   Answers: B D E

The features of obstructive jaundice are:

- icterus
- pain
- malaise
- loss of appetite
- pale stools and dark urine.

A raised bilirubin causes yellow discolouration of the skin and sclera. If a clotting disturbance occurs, bruising may be a feature.

Courvoisier's law states that in the presence of jaundice and a palpable gallbladder, jaundice is unlikely to be due to stones. (It is more likely to be due to tumour.)

Stones within the gallbladder cause fibrosis which results in a shrunken gallbladder which is scarred and therefore unable to dilate.

2.12 Hydatid disease   Answers: B C D E

Hydatid disease is due to *Echinococcus granulosus*. It is common in sheep-rearing areas. Man ingests the ova from earth on vegetables; the ova pass to the liver via the portal circulation and form cysts within the liver. These may be asymptomatic. The cyst wall may become calcified in which case it is visible on a plain abdominal X-ray. The clinical features include:

- obstructive jaundice
- malaise
- pruritis
- anaphylaxis.

The cyst may rupture into:

- the biliary tree producing cholangitis or jaundice
- the lung producing haemoptysis
- the peritoneum producing peritonitis
- the bowel and hence pass in the faeces.

Failed medical treatment, high risk of rupture or complications are the indications for surgery in which the cyst is excised.

2.13 Swelling at the angle of the jaw   Answers: B D

A pharyngeal pouch is a diverticulum of the pharynx occurring at the junction between the pharynx and the oesophagus. It is due to inco-ordination of the inferior constrictor muscle during swallowing which causes a rise in the pressure within the pharynx. This results in a bulge at a weak point. The typical symptom is regurgitation of undigested food. This may cause hoarseness of the voice. The pouch presses on the oesophagus and causes dysphagia and weight loss. Chest infections may occur if food is aspirated. A swelling is rare but if present it occurs low, behind the sternocleidomastoid muscle. The diagnosis is made on barium swallow. Treatment is by surgical excision.

Enlarged lymph nodes are the commonest cause of a lump in the neck. They are due to infection or neoplasia.

A thyroglossal cyst occurs in the midline along the thyroglossal tract. It moves on swallowing and on protrusion of the tongue.

A carotid body tumour arises in the chemoreceptor tissue at the carotid bifurcation, level with the hyoid bone. It occurs slightly lower than a branchial cyst. It is deep to the anterior edge of sternocleidomastoid muscle and may be pulsatile. It can be moved from side to side but not up and down. Treatment is by surgical removal.

Thyroid tissue tends to extend retrosternally, not towards the jaw.

2.14 Breast carcinoma   Answers: A D E

Breast carcinoma is the most common carcinoma in women. It commonly occurs in women aged over 40 years and the incidence increases with age. Only 1% of breast cancers occur in men. The aetiology is unknown. However, risk factors include:

- genetic factors – women with affected first-degree relatives (mother or sister) have increased susceptibility
- environmental – there is a geographical distribution, for example, low incidence in Japan
- increased risk – when one breast is affected the risk is increased in the contralateral breast
- nulliparous women and those having their first pregnancy over the age of 30 years; it is thought that oestrogens unopposed by progesterones increase susceptibility
- ionizing radiation
- obesity (oestrogens are produced in peripheral fat).

Protective factors:

- early first pregnancy
- breast feeding.

The incidence of breast carcinoma does not appear to be affected by the oral contraceptive pill.

2.15 Hydrocele   **Answers: B C**
A hydrocele is a serous collection of fluid within the *processus vaginalis*. It is idiopathic or due to trauma, infection or neoplasia. The clinical features are:

- scrotal swelling, usually without pain
- the cord is palpable above the swelling
- the testis is not palpable as it is surrounded by fluid
- it is fluctuant
- it is transilluminable
- it is irreducible.

Fertility is not affected.

The treatment is:

- aspiration (but fluid tends to recollect)
- surgical excision.

2.16 Scrotal swelling   **Answers: C D**

A hydrocoele envelops the testis and the testis is usually not palpable (see Paper 2, Question 15).

A strangulated inguinal hernia may occur in the scrotum but does not transilluminate.

An encysted hydrocoele of the cord in the scrotum is separate from the testis and transilluminates.

An epididymal cyst is fluid filled and separate from the testis. Therefore the testis is palpable separately.

Epididymal tuberculosis causes swelling confined to the scrotum; there is thickening of the cord which feels hard. It does not transilluminate.

2.17 Acute renal failure   **Answers: A B C**

Post-operatively renal failure develops in the following conditions:

- lack of renal perfusion, i.e. hypovolaemia due to haemorrhage or dehydration
- infection, especially Gram-negative septicaemia
- patients who have pre-existing renal disease.

An accurate fluid chart is required to monitor fluid balance. Frusemide or dopamine may be used to promote diuresis. Hyperkalaemia and acidosis occur.

A renal calculus is unlikely to cause acute renal failure post-operatively (as this would have to affect both kidneys) but obstruction of the ureter may result in hydronephrosis and reduced renal function.

2.18 Extradural haemorrhage   Answers: C

The classical history of an extradural haemorrhage is loss of consciousness with a 'lucid interval' before a deterioration in Glasgow coma scale. It is usually caused by damage of the middle meningeal artery. Haematoma develops between the dura and the skull raising intracranial pressure.

The lateralizing signs are an ipsilateral dilated pupil, and contralateral hemiparesis.

A skull fracture may not be present and there may not be a history of loss of consciousness.

Raised intracranial pressure causes a rise in blood pressure and a fall in heart rate. Treatment includes:

- mannitol (an osmotic diuretic)
- evacuation of haematoma via a burr hole or craniotomy.

2.19 Undescended testis   Answers: C D

An undescended testis lies anywhere along the course of descent from the abdomen to the scrotum. It is usually accompanied by a congenital inguinal hernia. Most cases are recognized in infancy or childhood and should be corrected early, if possible by the age of 2 years. An undescended testis predisposes to malignancy. The affected testis may be small and fertility may be impaired but if the other testis is functioning normally, this prevents sterility. There is an increased risk of torsion.

2.20 Varicocele   **Answers: C D E**
A varicocele is a collection of dilated veins of the pampiniform plexus. It is much more common on the left than on the right side. It is associated with renal tumours on the left side as this may obstruct drainage of the left testicular vein into the left renal vein.

The patient complains of a lump and/or an aching dull pain. A varicocele is likened to 'a bag of worms'. It is more noticeable when the patient is standing. It may be associated with infertility. Treatment is conservative, but in troublesome cases embolization can be performed. Alternatively, the veins can be ligated and divided.

2.21 Raynaud's phenomenon   **Answers: C E**
Raynaud's phenomenon describes certain changes of the hands or feet occurring in response to cold. Classically the fingers first turn white due to arterial spasm and the fingers become cold. Then they turn blue due to cyanosis and finally they turn red due to reactive hyperaemia; this is painful.

Raynaud's phenomenon may be idiopathic but it is associated with:

- a cervical rib
- cervical spondylosis
- connective tissue disorders, e.g. rheumatoid arthritis, CREST syndrome (i.e. calcinosis)
- Raynaud's phenomenon oesophagitis (note that

oesophagitis occurs and not oesophageal carcinoma)
- scleroderma
- telangiectasia
    use of vibratory tools
    arterial disease, e.g. atherosclerosis and emboli from the subclavian artery
    drugs, e.g. alpha receptor stimulants
    blood disorders, e.g. hyperviscosity.

2.22 Pancreatitis – complications   Answers: C E
The main complications of acute pancreatitis are:

- pseudocyst formation
- pancreatic abscess
- acute respiratory distress syndrome (ARDS)
- pleural effusions
- renal failure
- ileus – this is not due to obstruction
- shock – hypovolaemia and tachycardia
- diabetes mellitus
- metabolic effects – albumin falls, hypocalcaemia, hypomagnesaemia
- necrotizing haemorrhagic pancreatitis – fat necrosis can cause embolism; also calcium is sequestered
- haemorrhage – into a pseudocyst or due to peptic ulceration
- carcinoma of the pancreas and stones in the ampulla of Vater cause acute pancreatitis; also hyperparathyroidism, hypercalcaemia and hyperlipidaemia predispose to pancreatitis.

2.23 Basal cell carcinoma   Answer: B
A 'rodent ulcer' is a basal cell carcinoma. It characteristically presents on the upper part of the face and ears

especially on sun-exposed areas, but can occur on the neck or anywhere else on the body. It presents as a pearly white nodule with telangiectasia. As it enlarges, it may ulcerate with a pearly rolled edge.

Basal cell carcinomas do not metastasize. They are malignant by way of their local invasion and can cause significant tissue damage by eroding into local tissue.

Treatment:

- local excision
- radiotherapy (very effective)
- cryotherapy.

2.24 Recurrent fistulae   **Answers: A B C**
Infection in the ano-rectal region can lead to abscess or fistula formation. The causes of recurrent fistulae are:

- infection (e.g. tuberculosis)
- Crohn's disease (anal fissures are the most common anal lesion)
- neoplasia
- ulcerative colitis
- hydradenitis suppurativa.

Diverticulitis is a common cause of fistulae in the sigmoid colon but not of the anal canal. Remember that a fistula is an abnormal tract connecting two epithelial surfaces.

2.25 Abdominal pain/hypotension   **Answers: A C D**
Abdominal pain radiating to the back and presenting with 'shock' is a leaking abdominal aortic aneurysm until and unless proved otherwise (see Paper 1, Question 45).

There is often a history of collapse. The differential diagnosis is:

- acute pancreatitis
- mesenteric thrombosis
- myocardial infarction
- perforated peptic ulcer.

The history, examination and investigations clinch the diagnosis.

It is important to make the diagnosis of a leaking abdominal aortic aneurysm promptly as it presents a surgical emergency which requires immediate transfer to theatre. Obtain:

- intravenous access with two large bore cannulae
- blood for full blood count, urea and electrolytes, clotting screen, crossmatch of 10 units of blood.

Resuscitation should maintain blood pressure but avoid over-filling as this would increase the haemorrhage.

The patient requires a central line, urinary catheter and immediate surgery.

Renal colic typically presents with loin pain.

Acute appendicitis causes a localized peritonitis in the right iliac fossa. Shock occurs if the appendix perforates.

Pelvic inflammatory disease is unlikely to cause abdominal pain radiating to the back.

2.26 Tetany   **Answers: A B D**

Tetany is the muscle spasm that occurs in hypocalcaemia.

A metabolic alkalosis raises the pH as hydrogen ion concentration falls. This causes calcium to move into cells (hence the serum calcium level is reduced) and results in muscle twitching.

In thyroidectomy, a well-known complication is the removal of the parathyroid glands. This results in reduced parathyroid hormone and a fall in serum calcium.

A dirty wound causes tetanus, NOT tetany!

Over-breathing causes pCO_2 to fall, i.e. respiratory alkalosis. Hypocalcaemia occurs and the muscles become hyperexcitable.

Hypokalaemia is a recognized complication of paralytic ileus, not hypocalcaemia.

2.27 Ingrowing toe nail   **Answers: C D E**

An ingrowing toe nail occurs when the nail grows downwards into the soft tissue adjacent to it. It most commonly occurs on the lateral side of the big toe. It becomes infected and swollen causing pain and discomfort. The treatment is:

- to cut the nail square and keep it clean
- antibiotics are used in the acute stage for local infection
- surgical treatment includes wedge excision of the nail and nail bed OR avulsion of the nail and nail bed.

2.28 Upper gastrointestinal (GI) bleed   Answers: D E

Haematemesis of 1 litre is a medical emergency. Resuscitation is mandatory with attention to the airway, breathing and circulation.

Intravenous access is obtained and fluid loss is replaced with blood, colloid or crystalloid. Blood should be sent for a full blood count, urea and electrolytes, clotting screen and crossmatch. Pulse rate, blood pressure, and respiratory rate are monitored. (Hypovolaemia causes low blood pressure and tachycardia.) A central venous pressure line is useful to maintain fluid balance.

Gastroscopy is performed as soon as possible (within six hours), particularly in patients over 65 years, in patients who have a postural drop in blood pressure, where there is persistent tachycardia and when haemoglobin is < 10 g/dl.

Gastroscopy is performed to identify the source of the blood loss and facilitates treatment such as injection sclerotherapy. Surgery is indicated in persistent bleeding.

2.29 Pilonidal sinus   Answers: A D E

A pilonidal sinus is a sinus containing hairs. It commonly occurs in hair-bearing areas and may become infected to produce a pilonidal abscess. The commonest site is the natal cleft but it is also seen in the fingers of hairdressers where hairs become implanted under the skin. A pilonidal sinus tends to persist with chronic discharge via one or more sinuses to the skin. Treatment is by excision of the sinus with surrounding tissue.

2.30 Malignant melanoma   Answers: A B C

Malignant melanoma is a malignant tumour of melanocytes. It commonly occurs on the soles of the feet and on the head and neck. It can occur in the nail bed, eye or mouth.

Malignant melanoma is associated with exposure to ultraviolet light. The highest incidence is seen in Queensland, Australia. The incidence is lower in black populations.

Most tumours are pigmented but some have no pigment, i.e. they are amelanotic. Changes in the appearance of a mole should arouse suspicion. Malignant melanomas itch, bleed and ulcerate.

Some undergo spontaneous regression but this is not associated with hypophysectomy.

The treatment of choice is surgery with wide local excision of the lesion. Radiotherapy and chemotherapy are used for palliation in cases that have spread.

2.31 Buerger's disease   Answers: A B C E

Buerger's disease affects young men who smoke. It affects all limbs. The arteries become obliterated resulting in ischaemia to the affected areas. The veins and nerves are also affected. Patients present with peripheral ischaemic disease resulting in ulcers and digital gangrene. The treatment is to STOP SMOKING. Otherwise, progressive ischaemia occurs with gangrene, and amputation becomes necessary.

2.32 Carotid artery stenosis   Answers: A B D

Carotid artery occlusion usually occurs at the carotid bifurcation. It often goes unnoticed because the brain receives a contralateral blood supply via the circle of Willis.

Patients present with transient ischaemic attacks causing weakness in the contralateral limbs or *amaurosis fugax* which is a transient loss of vision in the ipsilateral eye. These resolve within a few hours. The cause is emboli from the carotid circulation impacting in smaller intracerebral vessels. Vomiting is not a sign of carotid disease. It would indicate disease of the posterior circulation. Patients with symptoms and stenosis greater than 75% should be treated with endarterectomy.

2.33 Anal fissure   Answers: A B D

The treatment of anal fissures may be:

- Conservative – with laxatives and local anaesthetic agents, some fissures heal spontaneously
- Surgical – this is either by 'anal dilatation' or 'lateral sphincterotomy'.

Surgery is indicated in cases of persistent fissures which become chronic. At surgery, examination under anaesthesia is performed to exclude other pathology. In Crohn's disease, sphincterotomy is not advised as there is a risk of sepsis.

2.34 Carpal tunnel syndrome   Answers: C D E

Carpal tunnel syndrome is due to compression of the median nerve in the carpal tunnel, deep to *flexor retinaculum*.

The median nerve supplies 'LOAF' muscles:

> **L**umbricals I & II
> **O**ponens pollicis
> **A**bductor pollicis brevis
> **F**lexor pollicis

These are the muscles of the thenar eminence.

Carpal tunnel syndrome causes wasting of the thenar eminence (the ulnar nerve supplies the muscles of the hypothenar eminence) and weakness of these muscles. Sensory loss occurs in the lateral 3½ fingers. Patients complain of paraesthesia especially in this distribution. There is pain in the forearm which is often worse at night.

On continuous tapping over the *Flexor retinaculum* the pain may be reproduced – this is Tinel's sign. Pain may also be reproduced by flexion of the wrist for 1–2 minutes, this is Phalen's sign.

Application of a tourniquet inflated to greater than arterial pressure may also reproduce the symptoms.

Surgical treatment involves division of the *Flexor retinaculum.*

2.35 Compound fracture of a bone   Answers: B C

A compound fracture is also known as an 'open fracture'. It is the fracture of a bone with breach of the overlying tissue allowing access to the exterior. This poses a major risk of infection.

The first-line treatment is:
• cover the wound with an iodine-soaked dressing

- antibiotic prophylaxis with penicillin and flucloxacillin
- tetanus immunization
- debridement
- skeletal stabilization.

Operative fixation may be carried out at this stage.

2.36 H₂ antagonists

Answers: A C D

Ranitidine is an H_2 antagonist. It acts by blocking the histamine receptors in the stomach thereby reducing gastric acid secretion. Cimetidine is another example. Both may be given orally or intravenously. They may be used immediately in upper gastrointestinal bleeding and are also useful in the prevention of stress ulcers of which there is risk in major operations.

2.37 Peptic ulcers

Answers: B C E

Peptic ulcers are ulcers of the stomach and duodenum.

The emergency complications are haemorrhage, perforation and pyloric stenosis.

Haemorrhage is due to erosion of the mucosa and blood vessel walls.

Perforation occurs when erosion of the bowel goes through the full thickness of the bowel wall.

Chronic ulceration may result in stricture formation due to fibrosis. This may occur in the body of the stomach, pylorus or duodenum.

Peptic ulcers are associated with:
- cigarette smoking

- stress
- genetic factors (e.g. where there is a family history)
- hyperparathyroidism – calcium levels are raised which stimulates gastric acid secretion.

Hyperparathyroidism presents with:
- abdominal pain
- bone disease:
    subperiosteal erosions visible on X-ray
    small lytic lesions of the skull = Pepperpot skull
    cystic lesions of bone
- renal calculi, i.e. 'Stones, bones and abdominal groans!'
- drugs, e.g. aspirin, steroids and non-steroidal anti-inflammatory drugs (NSAIDs)
- post-renal transplant
- Meckel's diverticulum – may have ectopic gastric mucosa which secretes gastrin
- Zollinger–Ellison syndrome.

2.38 Ulcerative colitis versus Crohn's disease

Answers: A D

Feature	Ulcerative colitis	Crohn's disease
Rectal bleeding	+ + +	+
Diarrhoea	+ + +	+
Steatorrhoea and malabsorption	–	+ + +
Rectal involvement	+ + +	+
Abdominal mass	+ /–	+ +
Perianal lesions	+ /–	+ + +
Fistulae	+ /–	+ + +
Toxic megacolon	+ +	+ /–
Malignant change	+ +	+ /–

2.39 Dupuytren's contracture   **Answers: A B**

Dupuytren's contracture (or cord) is a contracture of the palmar fascia. The cause is idiopathic but there is a familial component, i.e. autosomal dominant inheritance.

A flexor deformity of the finger develops which may be debilitating. It may occur bilaterally. Cord excision is indicated if it affects daily life.

2.40 Femoral shaft fracture   **Answers: A B D**

The femur is a large bone and its fracture involves a considerable amount of trauma. Blood loss into the surrounding soft tissue is significant and may result in shock. Intravenous fluid replacement is required.

In closed fractures, fat embolism (from bone marrow) is a common complication.

Tetanus immunization is mandatory in open fractures.

Internal fixation of the femur is by intramedullary nailing.

Healing of the femur takes at least three months.

2.41 Post-operative oliguria   **Answers: C D**

Urinary retention is a common post-operative complication occurring within 24 hours, especially in males. Examination of the abdomen is appropriate to look for an enlarged bladder. A urinary catheter may then be inserted and is diagnostic as well as therapeutic. Poor urine output may also be due to hypovolaemia. This is assessed with a fluid challenge of 200 ml given intravenously, which should raise urine output. If there is no response, 40 mg of frusemide (a loop diuretic) can be given. However, frusemide can be nephrotoxic and therefore care must be taken where renal failure is suspected. Persistent hypovolaemia causes acute renal failure. With rehydration, dopamine may be required to stimulate renal function. Mannitol is an osmotic diuretic and would not be appropriate. Haemodialysis can be used in the late stages.

2.42 Cellulitis   Answer: C

Cellulitis is inflammation of subcutaneous tissue which spreads locally. It is usually caused by *Streptococcus pyogenes*. The area of skin is typically red, hot and tender. Spreading cellulitis requires treatment with antibiotics, i.e. intravenous penicillin. Localized infection may produce a collection of pus in the form of an abscess which requires incision and drainage.

2.43 Meckel's diverticulum   Answers: B D E

Meckel's diverticulum is present in 2% of the population. It is the embryological remnant of the vitello-intestinal duct, and is situated on the ileum approximately two feet from the ileo-caecal junction. It is not the appendix.

Aide-mémoire:

RULE OF TWOs   (2%, 2 feet, and 2 inches long)

It may contain gastrin-secreting mucosa which stimulates acid secretion by the stomach and results in peptic ulceration.

If a Meckel's diverticulum becomes obstructed it gives rise to inflammation and presents with the features of acute appendicitis.

A Meckel's diverticulum may become inverted and cause intussusception which presents as small bowel obstruction.

2.44 Salivary duct calculi   Answers: B C D

The aetiology of salivary duct calculi is unknown. They are more common in the submandibular duct than in the parotid duct. (Acute inflammation of the salivary glands occurring in mumps is more common in the parotid gland.)

The calculi cause obstruction of the duct and stasis of saliva, with risk of infection. Clinically, the features are:

- painful swelling of the gland which is usually unilateral
- pain on eating meals as saliva production increases
- a foul taste in the mouth
- sudden relief of symptoms.

The standard investigations are plain X-rays and sialography. Submandibular duct calculi tend to be quite large and are therefore calcified. This shows up on X-ray. Parotid duct calculi however, tend to be small and are often radiolucent.

An ultrasound scan is useful to diagnose an abscess.

2.45 Carcinoma of the stomach   Answers: B C D E

Carcinoma of the stomach is common. It occurs in males more than females in a ratio of 2:1. It is most common in the antrum. It may occur as a result of malignant transformation of a polyp or as a primary lesion. The symptoms include epigastric pain, loss of appetite, loss of weight, dysphagia, regurgitation and vomiting. The patient appears cachectic. An epigastric mass may be palpable with tenderness and obstruction. Fluid in the stomach causes a succussion splash. There may be iron deficiency and/or pernicious anaemia. Metastases occur:

- by local invasion
- via lymphatics:
    to the liver causing ascites, hepatomegaly and jaundice
    to the lungs causing pleural effusions
    to the brain
    to lymph nodes (an enlarged lymph node in the left supraclavicular fossa is called Virchow's node or Troisier's sign)
- via the bloodstream
- by transcoelomic spread.

Metastases to the ovaries cause 'Krukenberg tumours'.

Surgical treatment is gastrectomy – total or partial, but the recurrence rate in the remnant is significant.

Prognosis depends on the extent of spread. In general, patients tend to present late and therefore prognosis is poor – a five-year survival rate of 10–25%.

2.46 Ureteric calculi   Answers: A D

The symptoms of ureteric calculi include loin pain which is colicky or constant, radiating into the groin and scrotum. The patient may roll about in pain with little relief. Microscopic or macroscopic haematuria occurs.

Approximately 70% of stones contain calcium oxalate; 15% are mixed phosphate stones; and 8% are uric acid.

'Triple phosphate' stones are composed of calcium,

magnesium and ammonium phosphate. This forms the typical 'staghorn calculus'. It is caused by the urease producing organism, Proteus.

Stone formation is increased in:

- hyperparathyroidism (increased calcium)
- gout
- cystinuria.

Urinary stasis predisposes to the precipitation of crystals and stone formation.

Infection producing alkaline urine causes the precipitation of calcium.

Schistosomiasis predisposes to bladder calculi.

Treatment includes:

- analgesia, e.g. diclofenac, for symptomatic relief
- lithotripsy
- ureteroscopic removal
- surgery.

Ureteric colic does not predispose to transitional cell carcinoma of the ureter.

Bladder calculi cause irritation and an increased incidence of bladder tumours of squamous cell type.

2.47 Metabolic response to trauma   Answers: B C E

Remember that trauma refers to all types of injury whether accidental or surgical. The physiological response occurs in two phases:

1. The EBB phase
This occurs in the first 24 hours. During this time there is:
- increased sympathetic activity
- increased acute phase proteins
- energy reserves are mobilized (glucose and triglyceride levels increase)
- insulin secretion decreases
- adrenocorticotrophin hormone (ACTH) increases; this causes a rise in cortisol levels and thus sodium and water retention with potassium loss
- release of antidiuretic hormone (ADH) to maintain blood pressure by fluid retention.

2. The FLOW phase
This occurs days to weeks later:
- metabolic rate is increased
- nitrogen excretion is increased due to protein catabolism – protein loss occurs from skeletal muscle breakdown resulting in loss of lean body mass
- energy is consumed
- insulin resistance occurs.

2.48 Rectal bleeding – bright red　　　　**Answers: B E**
The passage of bright red blood with the stool is usually due to local pathology.

Haemorrhoids are a common cause. However, a thrombosed pile consists of solid clot and altered blood which is dark red. Therefore, fresh red bleeding does not occur.

Anal fissure – constipation causes trauma to the fissure which opens up and causes bleeding.

Neoplasia, for example, adenoma or carcinoma of the rectum; these are situated close to the anal margin and can cause fresh red bleeding. More proximal colonic carcinoma would cause blood to be mixed in with the stool.

Trauma – local injury.

Note that the question specifies 'bright red blood' but there are numerous other causes of rectal bleeding (see also Paper 3, Question 45).

An ischiorectal abscess occurs in the ischiorectal fossa, the main symptom of which is pain.

2.49 Staging of breast carcinoma   Answers: A B

Staging of breast tumours is used to assess spread, predict prognosis and facilitate treatment.

Diagnosis is made by:

- ultrasound scan
- mammography
- FNA or biopsy
- lumpectomy.

Staging is done using the TNM classification, i.e.

- T = tumour size and extent (T_0-T_4)
- N = spread to lymph nodes (N_0-N_3)
- M = metastases (M_0 or M_1, indicating the presence or absence of metastases).

The Manchester system of staging is as follows:

STAGE	FEATURES	FIVE-YEAR SURVIVAL
I	Tumour ≤2 cm	85%
II	Tumour ≤5 cm Nodes not fixed	65%
III	Tumour ≤5 cm Supraclavicular nodes fixed	40%
IV	Distant metastases	10%

Treatment: in localized disease, i.e. for stages I and II, surgery is indicated. This includes wide local excision, axillary clearance, and adjuvant radiotherapy or chemotherapy.

If metastases are present, i.e. stages III and IV, treatment is palliative with radiotherapy and drugs, for example, tamoxifen, corticosteroids, and chemotherapy.

2.50 Hypocalcaemia   Answers: C D E

Calcium is present largely in bones; a small amount is present in blood, both as ions and bound to albumin. If acidity (H^+) increases, free calcium ions increase. Calcium levels must be corrected with respect to albumin as follows:

Corrected calcium = Measured calcium + (40–albumin) x 0.02

Calcium levels depend on intake and loss.

The causes of hypocalcaemia are:

- hypoparathyroidism
- chronic renal failure
- vitamin D deficiency
- septicaemia
- acute pancreatitis (gallstones can cause this).

In thyroidectomy, a complication is removal of the parathyroid glands which results in hypocalcaemia.

In low calcium states, replacement is with intravenous calcium gluconate.

In multiple myeloma and other malignancy, calcium levels tend to be raised. Parathyroid adenoma causes hypercalcaemia due to excess parathyroid hormone secretion.

50 questions: time allowed 2 hours.
Mark your answers with a tick (True) or a cross (False) in the box provided. Leave the box blank for 'Don't know'.
Do not look at the answers until you have completed the whole question paper.

3.1 Features consistent with a diagnosis of acute ulcerative colitis include

☐ A a normal barium enema   F
☐ B tachycardia > 100/minute   T
☐ C weight gain   F
☐ D serum albumin < 30 g/l   T
☐ E dilatation of the colon on plain abdominal X-ray   T

3.2 Which of the following occur in anterior perforation of peptic ulcers:

☐ A board-like rigidity   T
☐ B an increased area of liver dullness to percussion   F
☐ C a state of collapse dominating the picture shortly after onset   T
☐ D a chest X-ray in the erect position is often diagnostic   T
☐ E peritonitis is likely to follow   T

3.3 Adenomatous polyps

☐ A may be benign   T
☐ B may be malignant   T
☐ C should be left untreated if asymptomatic   F
☐ D of the tubular type in the colon are less likely to undergo malignant change than the villous type   T
☐ E may occur in Peutz–Jeghers syndrome   F

3.4 Crohn's disease

- ☐ A is associated with clubbing
- ☐ B may cause protein malabsorption
- ☐ C is characteristically associated with dilation of the terminal ileum
- ☐ D hardly ever affects the colon
- ☐ E may undergo spontaneous symptomatic remission

3.5 Which of the following symptoms and signs are suggestive of paralytic ileus:

- ☐ A abdominal distension
- ☐ B hyperactive bowel sounds
- ☐ C vomiting
- ☐ D colicky abdominal pain
- ☐ E gas and fluid dilated loops of small bowel on X-ray

3.6 Dysphagia

- ☐ A means difficulty in swallowing
- ☐ B means difficulty in speaking
- ☐ C may occur in a patient with a stroke
- ☐ D is associated with carcinoma of the oesophagus
- ☐ E occurs in pyloric stenosis

3.7 Diverticular disease of the colon

- ☐ A may present with pneumaturia
- ☐ B always occurs in the jejunum
- ☐ C is common in Western societies
- ☐ D may present with massive bleeding
- ☐ E is a causative factor in the development of carcinoma of the colon

3.8 A femoral hernia

- ☐ A should be treated with a truss
- ☐ B has the femoral vein lateral to it
- ☐ C may consist of omentum
- ☐ D appears above and medial to the inguinal ligament
- ☐ E can strangulate the bowel without obstructing it

3.9 In the radiological differentiation between cancer of the colon and diverticulitis, which of the following features would favour a diagnosis of diverticulitis:

- ☐ A a long segment of affected bowel
- ☐ B a gradual transition from normal to diseased bowel
- ☐ C evidence of spasm of the colon
- ☐ D a leak of barium through the bowel wall
- ☐ E a saw-toothed appearance

3.10 Sequelae of acute cholecystitis include

☐   A a perforation of the gallbladder
☐   B cholecystoduodenal fistula
☐   C ascending cholecystitis
☐   D an enlarged palpable gallbladder
☐   E septicaemia

3.11 Hepatitis B

☐   A is transmitted by the faeco-oral route
☐   B 'at risk' healthcare workers should receive immunization
☐   C predisposes to hepatocellular carcinoma
☐   D may cause liver cirrhosis
☐   E is a RNA virus

3.12 Ascending cholangitis is associated with

☐   A large bowel obstruction
☐   B gallstones
☐   C fever
☐   D stricture of the common bile duct
☐   E cholangiocarcinoma

3.13 Carcinoma of the oesophagus

☐   A   is diagnosed at colonoscopy
☐   B   presents with dysuria
☐   C   spreads to the liver
☐   D   can be treated with radiotherapy
☐   E   can be treated with surgery

3.14 A breast lump that is fixed to skin but not to deep tissues may be

☐   A   a fibroadenoma
☐   B   a cyst
☐   C   an intraduct papilloma
☐   D   an abscess
☐   E   fat necrosis

3.15 Clinical findings of a ruptured spleen may include

☐   A   haemorrhagic shock
☐   B   haematemesis
☐   C   reduced bowel sounds
☐   D   abdominal distension
☐   E   shifting dullness within the abdomen

3.16 Predisposing factors in the formation of renal calculi are

- ☐ A Dupuytren's contracture
- ☐ B a tropical climate
- ☐ C thyrotoxicosis
- ☐ D parathyroid tumour
- ☐ E malnutrition

3.17 In a case of abdominal trauma followed by haematuria

- ☐ A the kidney should be explored immediately
- ☐ B an intravenous urogram is of no value
- ☐ C an ultrasound scan of the abdomen should be obtained
- ☐ D nephrectomy may be required
- ☐ E the patient must be followed up

3.18 Regarding ulcerative colitis

- ☐ A malignancy is a feature
- ☐ B transmural involvement occurs
- ☐ C rectum is always involved
- ☐ D it is familial
- ☐ E crypt abscesses are seen

3.19 A direct inguinal hernia

☐ A is usually congenital
☐ B may contain bowel, omentum or bladder
☐ C may occur with an indirect hernia
☐ D protrudes through the posterior wall of the inguinal canal lateral to the inferior epigastric vessels
☐ E has a high risk of strangulation

3.20 Recognized complications of venous insufficiency of the lower limb include

☐ A chronic ulceration
☐ B superficial phlebitis
☐ C stiffness of the ankle joint
☐ D deep vein thrombosis
☐ E localized eczema

3.21 Digital gangrene may be caused by

☐ A frost bite
☐ B alcoholism
☐ C ergot derivatives
☐ D polyneuritis
☐ E cervical rib

3.22 In pancreatitis

- ☐ A antibiotics are mandatory
- ☐ B the clinical picture is a reliable indicator of prognosis
- ☐ C treatment is conservative
- ☐ D laparotomy may be indicated
- ☐ E a rise in serum amylase is diagnostic

3.23 A carbuncle

- ☐ A is associated with glycosuria
- ☐ B is commonly found on the palm of the hand
- ☐ C is commonly found on the neck
- ☐ D forms an area of necrosis with multiple sinuses
- ☐ E is best treated with systemic antibiotics

3.24 An anal fissure

- ☐ A is associated with a sentinel pile
- ☐ B most commonly lies anteriorly
- ☐ C is an ulcer of the rectal mucosa
- ☐ D is a cause of bleeding in infancy
- ☐ E is a recognized complication of Crohn's disease

3.25 The effect of an arterial embolus depends on

☐   A   collateral circulation of the area where the embolus lodges
☐   B   site of origin
☐   C   size of the embolus
☐   D   composition of the embolus
☐   E   time of onset of thrombolysis

3.26 Coronary artery grafting for ischaemic heart disease

☐   A   routinely requires cardiopulmonary bypass
☐   B   is usually performed using intercostal arteries as grafts
☐   C   is unlikely to be successful if more than two major coronary arteries are narrowed
☐   D   requires preceding coronary angiography
☐   E   has not been shown to prolong life

3.27 The following are proven methods of prophylaxis in reducing the incidence of deep vein thrombosis:

☐   A   pneumatic calf compression during operation
☐   B   subcutaneous low molecular weight heparin daily
☐   C   elasticated compression stockings
☐   D   aspirin 300 mg four times a day
☐   E   immobilization

3.28 Surgical emphysema may be caused by

☐   A   spontaneous pneumothorax
☐   B   perforation of the oesophagus
☐   C   hyperventilation
☐   D   traumatic pneumothorax
☐   E   smoking

3.29 Anal pain occurs in

☐   A   carcinoma of the anal canal
☐   B   first-degree haemorrhoids
☐   C   fissure *in ano*
☐   D   anal warts
☐   E   perianal haematoma

3.30 The following apply to malignant melanoma:

☐   A   they usually arise from a pre-existing mole
☐   B   prognosis depends on the depth of invasion
☐   C   prognosis is worse in the superficial spreading form
           than in the nodular form
☐   D   prognosis is worse in amelanotic lesions
☐   E   they metastasize to regional lymph nodes

3.31 The following are features of peripheral arterial disease:

- ☐ A intermittent claudication
- ☐ B transient ischaemic attacks
- ☐ C diabetes mellitus
- ☐ D rest pain
- ☐ E critical ischaemia

3.32 Infection with tuberculosis produces

- ☐ A a hot red abscess
- ☐ B granuloma formation
- ☐ C collapse of vertebral bodies
- ☐ D epididymitis
- ☐ E frequency of micturition

3.33 Carcinoma of the tongue

- ☐ A is associated with constipation
- ☐ B usually occurs on the posterior third
- ☐ C is associated with the presence of leukoplakia
- ☐ D is usually an adenocarcinoma
- ☐ E may be treated by radiotherapy

3.34 A prolapsed lumbar intervertebral disc

- ☐ A presents with arm pain
- ☐ B may cause urinary retention
- ☐ C at the level of L3/4 may result in an absent knee jerk
- ☐ D presents with buttock pain
- ☐ E may be treated conservatively

3.35 Metastases in bone are a common feature of carcinoma of the

- ☐ A kidney
- ☐ B rectum
- ☐ C lungs
- ☐ D stomach
- ☐ E thyroid

3.36 Heparin

- ☐ A is given intravenously for the prophylaxis of deep vein thrombosis
- ☐ B may cause osteomalacia
- ☐ C is reversible with protamine
- ☐ D has a half-life of 12 hours
- ☐ E action is monitored by the international normalized ratio

3.37 Regarding an intertrochanteric fracture of the femur

☐   A it is common in young men
☐   B the leg is shortened and externally rotated
☐   C it is treated with internal fixation
☐   D there is a high risk of avascular necrosis of the head of the femur
☐   E it should be treated with total hip replacement

3.38 Concerning antibiotics

☐   A a cephalosporin is used prophylactically in cholecystectomy
☐   B a complete course should be given for prophylaxis in surgery
☐   C they are the treatment of choice for an abscess
☐   D prophylaxis is advised for surgery in patients with prosthetic heart valves
☐   E prophylaxis is recommended in colorectal surgery

3.39 Which of the following complicates the passage of a urinary catheter into the bladder:

☐   A renal stones
☐   B pyelonephritis
☐   C septicaemia
☐   D prostatitis
☐   E urethral bleeding

3.40 Hyperhidrosis

☐   A   is dryness of the skin
☐   B   is associated with an increase in the number of eccrine glands
☐   C   does not occur in the palms
☐   D   can be eliminated with sympathectomy
☐   E   classically affects young women

3.41 Before starting an urgent operation for large bowel obstruction which of the following investigations should be carried out:

☐   A   full blood count
☐   B   chest X-ray
☐   C   barium enema
☐   D   sigmoidoscopy
☐   E   electrolyte concentrations in serum

3.42 Pseudomembranous colitis

☐   A   is caused by *Clostridium perfringens*
☐   B   may occur after only one dose of an antibiotic
☐   C   may occur weeks after antibiotic treatment
☐   D   may occur after treatment with metronidazole
☐   E   is treated with intravenous metronidazole

3.43 In the first 12 hours following a major abdominal operation, particular attention should be paid to

- ☐ A urinary output
- ☐ B pupil size
- ☐ C wound drainage
- ☐ D respiration
- ☐ E core temperature

3.44 Regarding total parenteral nutrition

- ☐ A it is beneficial for most malnourished patients pre-operatively
- ☐ B it is beneficial for malnourished patients post-operatively
- ☐ C it is usually given via a peripheral intravenous line
- ☐ D there is a risk of sepsis
- ☐ E it can be given via a nasogastric tube

3.45 Blood may be found on the glove following rectal examination in

- ☐ A diverticulitis
- ☐ B Meckel's diverticulum
- ☐ C carcinoma of the oesophagus
- ☐ D intussusception
- ☐ E chronic prostatitis

3.46 Thyroid carcinoma

☐ A of the papillary type usually affects young adults
☐ B presents as a lump in the neck that moves on swallowing
☐ C of the anaplastic type carries the best prognosis
☐ D medullary carcinoma is of parafollicular cells
☐ E typically causes thyroid dysfunction

3.47 Regarding kidney transplant

☐ A it is only offered to patients less than 50 years of age
☐ B the transplant is placed extraperitoneally
☐ C urine output is monitored to detect rejection
☐ D immunosuppression is required
☐ E a urinary tract infection is a contraindication

3.48 The causes of stricture of the bowel include

☐ A gluten enteropathy
☐ B slow release potassium tablets
☐ C mesenteric ischaemia
☐ D Crohn's disease
☐ E Peutz–Jeghers syndrome

3.49 The level of amylase in serum is typically raised in patients with

- ☐ A acute pancreatitis
- ☐ B acute appendicitis
- ☐ C renal failure
- ☐ D perforated peptic ulcer
- ☐ E acute cholecystitis

3.50 Volvulus

- ☐ A causes venous infarction of the bowel
- ☐ B causes peritonitis
- ☐ C can be cured by performing a barium enema
- ☐ D occurs only in the sigmoid colon
- ☐ E commonly occurs in children and young adults

———————————— **END** ————————————

Go over your answers until your time is up.
Correct answers and teaching notes are overleaf.

The correct answer options for each question are given below.

3.1	B D E	3.26	A D
3.2	A C D E	3.27	A B C
3.3	A B D	3.28	B D
3.4	A B E	3.29	A C E
3.5	A C E	3.30	B D E
3.6	A C D	3.31	A B D E
3.7	A C D	3.32	B C D E
3.8	B C E	3.33	C E
3.9	A C D E	3.34	B C D E
3.10	A B D E	3.35	A C E
3.11	B C D	3.36	C
3.12	B C D E	3.37	B C
3.13	C D E	3.38	A D E
3.14	D E	3.39	C D E
3.15	A C D E	3.40	D E
3.16	B D E	3.41	A B E
3.17	C D E	3.42	B C D
3.18	A C E	3.43	A C D E
3.19	B C	3.44	B D
3.20	A B C E	3.45	A B D
3.21	A C E	3.46	A B D
3.22	C D	3.47	B C D E
3.23	A C D E	3.48	B C D
3.24	A D E	3.49	A C D E
3.25	A C D E	3.50	A B C

3.1 Ulcerative colitis   **Answers: B D E**
Ulcerative colitis presents with recurrent exacerbations of colonic inflammation. This causes diarrhoea, rectal bleeding and abdominal pain. It may lead to dehydration, fever, hypotension and tachycardia. Dilatation of the bowel may result in toxic megacolon and this may eventually perforate and cause peritonitis. Weight loss is common. Profuse diarrhoea with blood loss causes a fall in albumin. (See also Paper 3, Question 18.)

3.2 Perforated peptic ulcer   **Answers: A C D E**
Perforation of a peptic ulcer is more commonly anterior than posterior. Duodenal ulcer perforation is more common than gastric ulcer perforation.

There may be a history of non-steroidal inflammatory drug ingestion.

An erect chest X-ray shows gas under the diaphragm and this is detected clinically by resonance to percussion over the liver. It can be confirmed with a contrast study.

The typical presentation is of sudden onset epigastric pain with vomiting.

There is rebound tenderness, guarding, board-like rigidity and cardiovascular collapse.

Posterior perforations tend to occur into the lesser sac which causes the peritonitis to remain localized.

3.3 Colonic polyps   **Answers: A B D**
A polyp is an abnormal growth of epithelium. It may be

pedunculated (on a stalk) or sessile (broad based and flat).

Adenoma describes a benign growth which appears tubular, villous or tubulo-villous. In the large bowel all types are pre-malignant. The villous type has the greatest potential for malignant change and is most often sessile, whereas the tubular type has the least potential for malignant change and is sessile or pedunculated. (The tubulo-villous type lies in between.)

Peutz–Jeghers syndrome is an autosomal dominant inherited condition. Numerous polyps occur in the small bowel. These are hamartomas and not adenomas. Spots of brown pigmentation may occur on the lips.

3.4 Crohn's disease   **Answers: A B E**

Crohn's disease and ulcerative colitis are inflammatory bowel diseases. Both are associated with clubbing. Crohn's disease affecting the small bowel may result in malabsorption of:

- iron (iron deficiency anaemia) – absorbed in the duodenum
- vitamin B12 (pernicious anaemia) – absorbed in the ileum
- folate – absorbed in the jejunum
- protein (malnutrition)
- fat (steatorrhoea)
- bile salts – (gall stone formation) absorbed in the terminal ileum
- fat-soluble vitamins, i.e. vitamins A, D, E, K.

Crohn's disease commonly affects the terminal ileum

producing a 'terminal ileitis'. Inflammation results in narrowing. It affects the colon in about 25% of cases. It also affects the perianal region. The natural history is of chronic inflammatory disease with periods of relapse and remission.

3.5 Paralytic ileus   **Answers: A C E**

In paralytic ileus, the bowel is quiescent and there is a functional obstruction of the bowel. This results in dilation of the bowel and vomiting. The signs are:

- inspection – abdominal distension
- palpation – tenderness which may be mild or even absent
- percussion – hyperresonant
- auscultation – absent bowel sounds

Colicky abdominal pain does not occur as there is no mechanical obstruction and the bowel is not contracting. X-rays show dilated loops of bowel with gas and fluid levels.

3.6 Dysphagia   **Answers: A C D**

Dysphagia is difficulty in swallowing. Do not confuse this with dysphasia which is impaired speech. Dysphagia occurs when there is an obstruction to the passage of solids or fluids in the oesophagus. Obstruction may be:

- in the lumen, e.g. carcinoma of the oesophagus
- in the oesophageal wall, e.g. benign stricture, carcinoma, pharyngeal pouch, leiomyoma, etc
- outside the wall, e.g. carcinoma of the bronchus producing compression
- disorder of motility, e.g. achalasia, stroke.

3.7 Diverticular disease   **Answers: A C D**
Diverticular disease is a common condition in Western society caused by lack of fibre in the diet. It is asymptomatic. Inflammation of a diverticulum is 'diverticulitis'. It can occur in the small bowel but is far more common in the colon. It is not associated with malignancy. The complications and their presentations are listed below.

Complications	Presentations
Inflammation	Left iliac fossa pain
Inflammation/ haemorrhage	Rectal bleeding
Infection/sepsis/ abscess formation	Swinging pyrexia with abdominal pain
Perforation	'Rigid abdomen'
Fistulae	Pneumaturia
Stricture formation	Bowel obstruction with distension, vomiting etc

3.8 Femoral hernia   **Answers: B C E**
Although a truss may be useful, elective surgery for a femoral hernia is advised. It should be arranged at the earliest opportunity because femoral hernias have a high risk of strangulation.

Femoral hernias consist of omentum, fat, lymph nodes or bowel.

The anatomy is: femoral nerve; artery; vein; and femoral canal from lateral to medial.

A femoral hernia appears below the inguinal ligament and lateral to the pubic tubercle.

Like any bowel hernia it can strangulate without obstruction (see Paper 1, Question 8).

3.9 X-ray features of carcinoma of the colon versus diverticular disease　　　　　**Answers: A C D E**
On a barium enema, carcinoma of the colon presents as an apple core stricture, with shouldering.

Obstruction results in dilation proximal to the stricture.

In contrast, diverticular disease is seen as numerous pockets – a saw-tooth appearance is due to numerous diverticulae. A stricture in this case tends to affect a long segment of bowel and there may be spasm. Obstruction can also occur.

In both conditions, an abscess may appear as a gas bubble and if perforation occurs there may be gas under the diaphragm.

3.10 Acute cholecystitis　　　　　**Answers: A B D E**
Inflammation of the gallbladder may spread along the cystic and bile ducts towards the liver causing ascending cholangitis, not cholecystitis (read the question carefully!) The inflammation may be chemical or infective due to *Escherichia coli* in the gastrointenstinal tract.

If the gallbladder becomes infected it may fill with pus to form an empyema. Septicaemia may then ensue. Mucus secretion in the gallbladder may cause a mucocoele which is palpable as an enlarged gallbladder.

Necrosis and gangrene may result in perforation of the gallbladder producing a peritonitis.

If the gallbladder perforates into a part of the bowel a cholecystoenteric fistula is created. Gallstones may then pass directly into the bowel and a gallstone ileus may result.

3.11 Hepatitis B   Answers: B C D
Hepatitis B virus is a DNA virus. It has an incubation period of 2–6 months. It is transmitted in blood products, for example, by intravenous drug users, blood transfusions, etc. Healthcare workers who are at risk of needle stick injuries or other injuries should be immunized with a course of three vaccinations. The clinical features include anorexia, malaise, nausea and vomiting. Jaundice and abdominal pain may occur. Liver function is affected and therefore clotting abnormalities may occur. Hepatitis B causes chronic hepatitis with an increased risk of cirrhosis and hepatocellular carcinoma.

3.12 Ascending cholangitis   Answers: B C D E
Ascending cholangitis is characterized by pain, pyrexia and jaundice. Obstruction of the bile ducts due to gallstones, bile duct stricture or carcinoma predisposes to infection which ascends into the intrahepatic ducts. It may result in liver abscess. Invasive procedures, for example, stent insertion, may introduce infection and cause cholangitis.

3.13 Carcinoma of the oesophagus   Answers: C D E
The classical presentation is dysphagia.

Investigations include a barium swallow; oesophago-gastroduodenoscopy (OGD) is ideal as biopsies can be taken if tumour is seen. CT scan is then useful to determine the extent of spread and to assess operability. Spread is local, to local lymph nodes and to the liver and lungs.

Radiotherapy is useful for squamous carcinoma.

Surgery is used for adenocarcinoma.

Chemotherapy is not routinely used.

3.14 Breast lump   Answers: D E

The skin changes in breast disease are often very marked. Tethering of the skin or dimpling is suggestive of carcinoma. Fixation to the skin or deeper tissue also suggests carcinoma.

Peau d'orange is pathognomonic of carcinoma.

If a lump is present, its characteristics (i.e. surface and texture) provide useful information.

Fibroadenoma usually produces a discrete lump with a smooth surface. It may be cystic. It is not fixed to the skin or deeper tissue.

A lipoma is a soft mobile lump.

An abscess affects the skin and subcutaneous tissue. It is red, hot and tender. Collection of pus makes it fluctuant and it may point and then discharge. It is fixed to the skin which may then become indurated.

Fat necrosis occurs following trauma to the breast. It forms a hard lump which is fixed to the skin.

3.15 Splenic rupture   **Answers: A C D E**

A ruptured spleen presents with pain, tenderness and guarding in the left upper quadrant of the abdomen. Pain may be referred to the left shoulder. There is usually a history of trauma.

The signs of internal haemorrhage are:

* hypotension/hypovolaemia peritonitis producing an ileus (if haemorrhage occurs into the peritoneal cavity)
* abdominal distension
* shifting dullness due to blood within the peritoneal cavity
* fixed dullness may occur due to extraperitoneal blood loss

Haematemesis does not occur as bleeding is not within the bowel.

The diagnosis may be confirmed by ultrasound scan or CT scan.

Splenic rupture is treated by splenectomy with attention to vaccination and penicillin prophylaxis (see Paper 1, Question 12).

3.16 Renal calculi   **Answers: B D E**

Most renal calculi are idiopathic. The following factors predispose to their formation:

- stagnation of urine – congenital or acquired (obstruction)
- infection, for example, urease-producing organisms such as Proteus
- dehydration/malnutrition
- raised calcium, for example, hyperparathyroidism, immobility
- gout – uric acid
- hyperoxaluria – calcium oxalate
- cysteinuria – cysteine stones

3.17 Renal trauma   **Answers: C D E**

Injury to the kidney commonly results in localized pain and haematuria. Haematuria may be macroscopic or microscopic. Hypotension may occur.

Appropriate investigations include:

- intravenous urogram
- ultrasound scan
- CT scan
- arteriography.

Treatment is usually conservative. Close monitoring of urine output, pulse rate and blood pressure is required.

The patient should be followed up for several months following renal trauma as complications such as hypertension or renal failure may develop late. There may be persistent bleeding. This may necessitate nephrectomy.

3.18 Ulcerative colitis   Answers: A C E

Ulcerative colitis is an inflammatory bowel disease (along with Crohn's disease, amoebiasis, etc.) affecting the colon. The aetiology is unknown but genetic and environmental factors have been implicated.

It is a mucosal disease which involves the rectum and spreads proximally. There is inflammation of the mucosa, crypt abscesses and goblet cell depletion. Pseudopolyps occur where intact mucosa appears raised adjacent to ulcerated mucosa.

In patients with pancolitis the risk of malignancy is significant and total colectomy is advised.

3.19 Direct hernia   Answers: B C

Inguinal hernias occur above and medial to the pubic tubercle. A direct inguinal hernia is NOT controlled by pressure on the internal (deep) ring. An indirect inguinal hernia is controlled (after reduction) by pressure on the internal ring.

A direct inguinal hernia is due to weakness of the posterior wall of the inguinal canal such that the abdominal contents bulge forward. An indirect inguinal hernia is the passage of abdominal contents along the inguinal canal towards the scrotum. The two can occur together.

A direct inguinal hernia lies medial to the inferior epigastric vessels, whereas an indirect inguinal hernia lies lateral to them.

The risk of strangulation is low in a direct hernia.

3.20 Complications of venous insufficiency

Answers: A B C E

Chronic venous insufficiency causes:

- ankle flare due to venous hypertension
- dilated calf 'blow outs' due to incompetent valves
- superficial thrombophlebitis
- eczema
- pigmentation of the skin, usually over the medial aspect of the ankle; this may spread over the lower leg
- the skin may break down and ulcerate, especially over the medial malleolus; this may become infected and very painful; rarely, an ulcer undergoes malignant change, i.e. into a squamous cell carcinoma; this is called a Marjolin's ulcer
- lipodermatosclerosis may occur; the skin becomes red, hot and tender
- subcutaneous fibrosis causes stiffness of the ankle joint which may cause fixed flexion.

Venous insufficiency is a complication of deep vein thrombosis.

3.21 Digital gangrene

Answers: A C E

Digital gangrene is caused by obstruction of blood flow to the tips of the fingers. It occurs in peripheral arterial disease. The causes include:

- digital artery embolism, for example, from the heart in atrial fibrillation or from a subclavian artery with atherosclerosis
- thrombus formation
- cervical rib: pressure on the sympathetic nerves may cause vasoconstriction; direct pressure on the subclavian artery would reduce blood flow

- frostbite – where severe vasoconstriction causes hypoxia
- blood disorders, for example, cold agglutinins
- vasculitis with vasospasm
- Raynaud's phenomenon
- drugs, for example, ergot derivatives or beta-blockers.

3.22 Pancreatitis   Answers: C D

The treatment of pancreatitis depends on the severity of the attack.

The patient is given intravenous fluids and kept nil by mouth.

If there are signs of infection, antibiotics are given.

A nasogastric tube is inserted.

A urinary catheter is inserted to monitor urine output.

A central venous pressure (CVP) line may be required to control fluid balance.

Blood pressure and heart rate are monitored.

Analgesia is given as required.

For respiratory problems, oxygen is given via a mask; ventilation may be necessary. There is a risk of acute respiratory distress syndrome (ARDS).

Surgery is not the treatment of choice in acute pancreatitis.

The clinical picture in acute pancreatitis can be very deceptive.

In chronic pancreatitis, if the pancreatic tissue is severely damaged it is unable to mount a response and therefore a rise in serum amylase does not occur. Hence, a 'normal' amylase level is seen when there is considerable pathology.

Other conditions which cause a rise in amylase include perforated peptic ulcers and trauma.

Essentially, the treatment is conservative. Laparotomy may be required for debridement of severe necrosis as a last resort.

3.23 Carbuncle   Answers:A C D E

A carbuncle is a widespread infection of the hair follicles and subcutaneous tissue caused by *Staphylococcus aureus*. It affects the adjacent skin and multiple sinuses develop. The back of the neck is commonly affected. It is more common in diabetics, hence the association with glycosuria. Treatment is with flucloxacillin.

3.24 Anal fissure   Answers: A D E

Definition: an anal fissure is a longitudinal tear of the anal mucosa. It is exquisitely painful and patients often refuse ano-rectal examination. Defaecation causes pain with prolonged burning and impairs healing. The most common site is the posterior anal margin. It occurs in infants, children and adults.

Externally, there may be a skin tag called a sentinel pile.

The anal sphincter may increase in tone causing constipation and bleeding which is detected as a smear on the toilet paper. There may also be pruritus.

Associated conditions are Crohn's disease, ulcerative colitis and tuberculosis.

3.25 Arterial embolus   Answers: A C D E

Definition: an embolus is the passage of a mass carried in the circulation. It produces its effects by lodging in smaller vessels and preventing oxygen and nutrients from reaching the tissues.

The different types of emboli include:

- thrombus – this is the most common
- fat – seen in fractures
- air – occurs in neck trauma
- nitrogen – caissons disease.

The management of emboli is:

- anti-coagulation to prevent extension and further recurrence
- thrombolysis – this is useful in patients who are at risk of surgery
- surgical embolectomy.

The site of origin varies; commonly it arises in the heart and is caused by atrial fibrillation. It is the site where the embolus lodges rather than its site of origin that determines its effects. The size of the embolus will determine the site of impact and therefore its effects. The main effect of an embolus is ischaemia. Hence, the presence of a collateral circulation may allow the tissue to remain viable.

Infection of an embolus, for example, an embolus of vegetations from the heart, can lodge in an artery and cause a mycotic aneurysm.

3.26 Coronary artery bypass graft   **Answers: A D**

Coronary artery surgery is performed on cardiopulmonary bypass. It is performed using the left internal mammary artery or a saphenous vein. Three- or four-vessel disease produces marked symptoms and hence surgery is very successful in relieving symptoms.

Investigations required prior to operation include:

- chest X-ray
- electrocardiogram (ECG)
- exercise ECG
- coronary angiography.

The operative mortality is 2–3%. In addition to the general complications, specific complications include strokes, neurological deficit and graft failure.

Surgery provides:

- reduced morbidity with relief of symptoms in most cases
- reduced mortality.

In patients with three- or four-vessel disease and severe symptoms, such as unstable angina, the mortality is reduced following operation. However, in patients with one- or two-vessel disease, mortality is not improved by operation.

3.27 Deep vein thrombosis (DVT) prophylaxis

Answers:A B C

There is a significant risk of DVT post-operatively.

Pre-disposing factors include trauma, surgery, dehydration, immobilization, malignancy, polycythaemia and the oral contraceptive pill. The risk is higher following major operations.

Measures used to prevent DVT are:

- minimal trauma to the legs during handling of the patient
- rehydration – increased blood viscosity predisposes to thrombosis
- heparin (subcutaneous 5000 i.u. twice daily)
- elasticated compression stockings
- pneumatic calf stockings during operations
- early mobilization
- warfarin – but there is a risk of haemorrhage
- intravenous dextran.

3.28 Surgical emphysema

Answers: B D

Surgical emphysema is due to air tracking into subcutaneous tissues. Clinically there is swelling of the affected area with crepitus. It may be visible on X-ray.

The causes are trauma and oesophageal rupture. Treatment is of the underlying cause. The surgical emphysema itself tends to resolve.

3.29 Anal pain

Answers: A C E

Lesions in the anal canal can present with pain.

Carcinoma can cause ulceration with bleeding and pain.

Perianal haematoma causes a localized inflammatory reaction which is painful.

Haemorrhoids are not painful *per se,* but it is their complications which cause pain; first-degree haemorrhoids are internal and not painful.

Anal warts cause irritation and discomfort; they do not produce pain.

Fissure *in ano* is classically very painful, as can be fistula *in ano,* especially when infection occurs.

A perianal abscess causes pain and discomfort, especially on sitting.

3.30 Malignant melanoma   Answers: B D E

Most malignant melanomas arise in normal skin. Only a minority arise in a pre-existing mole. Prognosis depends on depth of invasion. There are two classifications used to determine prognosis:

- Clarke's level of invasion is based on the layer of skin penetrated – if the basement membrane is not penetrated the prognosis is good, whereas invasion into the subcutaneous fat has a very poor prognosis.
- Breslow's classification uses the thickness of the tumour to predict prognosis:

Depth of invasion (mm)	Risk
0.76	Low
0.76–1.5	Moderate
>1.5	High

Most lesions are of the superficial spreading type. These have a better prognosis than the nodular type which invade in depth.

Amelanotic lesions have a worse prognosis. This may be because they are diagnosed late or because they are inherently more aggressive.

Malignant melanomas spread via lymphatics to the regional lymph nodes, and via the blood stream to the lungs, liver and brain.

3.31 Peripheral arterial disease (PAD)   **Answers: A B D E**
Intermittent claudication is a sign of chronic lower limb ischaemia. As this worsens it develops into rest pain and critical ischaemia. Critical ischaemia is arterial disease which threatens the viability of the foot or leg. It usually occurs gradually but can develop suddenly if there is thrombus or embolus occluding a vessel.

In acute critical ischaemia of the foot the classical features are the six Ps:

Pain
Pallor
Pulseless

Paraesthesia (numbness of the foot)
Paralysis (this is a late sign)
Perishing with cold.

Transient ischaemic attacks are a feature of ischaemic events in the brain which may result from carotid artery emboli.

Diabetes mellitus is associated with atherosclerosis. However, it is not a feature of PAD. Also, diabetic neuropathy results in injury and ulceration of the feet due to poor healing.

3.32 Tuberculosis   Answers: B C D E

The incidence of tuberculosis (TB) is increasing in the UK. It is caused by *Mycobacterium tuberculosis* which can affect the lungs, bones, gastrointestinal tract, urinary tract and skin. It is characterized by granuloma formation and caseating necrosis. Pus forms slowly and results in the formation of an abscess. As the abscess forms slowly and there is no redness/inflammation, it is called a 'cold abscess'.

Infection of the spine can be devastating. It affects both the bone and the intervertebral disc spaces. Vertebral collapse may cause spinal cord compression which requires surgical intervention.

TB spreads via the blood stream to the genito-urinary tract. Tuberculous epididymitis causes swelling of the scrotum, but symptoms may be mild and go unnoticed.

TB affecting the urinary tract causes frequency of micturition as is seen in bacterial urinary tract infection.

3.33 Carcinoma of the tongue   Answers: C E

Carcinoma of the tongue occurs most commonly on the anterior two-thirds of the tongue. It is more common in males than females. There is an association with pipe smoking, alcohol, leukoplakia, betel nut chewing and poor oral hygiene.

The presentation is of a nodule or ulcer. The tongue is covered in squamous epithelium and therefore carcinoma is squamous in type.

Spread occurs locally or by lymphatic drainage to the sub-mental and cervical lymph nodes.

Prognosis depends on spread. If metastasis has occurred, the five-year survival rate is only 18%.

Definitive treatment is by surgery, radiotherapy or both.

3.34 Prolapsed lumbar disc   Answers: B C D E

A prolapsed lumbar disc classically presents with back pain radiating to the buttock. There may be paraesthesia of the leg and muscle weakness.

At the affected level, reflexes are diminished, for example, L3/4 – knee jerk; L5/S1 – ankle jerk. *Cauda equina* compression may cause urinary retention.

Treatment of a prolapsed disc is by the three Rs:
  Rest
  Removal
  Rehabilitation.

Improvement may occur following rest alone.

3.35 Bone metastases   **Answers: A C E**

This is a list well worth committing to memory. Tumours commonly metastasizing to bone include:

- breast
- thyroid
- bronchus
- prostate – remember that this causes sclerotic lesions
- kidney

Lesions are lytic (except prostate) and present as pathological fractures.

3.36 Heparin   **Answer: C**

Heparin inhibits blood coagulation by inactivation of thrombin and coagulation factors VII, IX, X, XI, XII. Intermittent subcutaneous injection is given for prophylaxis of venous thrombosis (5000 i.u. twice daily). Intravenous therapy is given for the treatment of deep vein thrombosis.

Heparin has a short half-life of about one hour. It is reversible with protamine. The best test for monitoring therapy is activated partial thromboplastin time (APTT).

The internationalized ratio (INR) is a measure of prothrombin time which is used to monitor warfarin activity.

Long-term heparin therapy causes osteoporosis.

3.37 Intertrochanteric fracture of the femur   **Answers:B C**

Intertrochanteric fractures of the femur occur in the elderly, especially in women who have osteoporosis and are predisposed to weak bones. The fracture may be traumatic or pathological. The classical presentation is shortening of the leg and external rotation.

Intertrochanteric fractures are extracapsular. Therefore, they unite early with little risk of avascular necrosis. Treatment is by internal fixation to allow early mobilization.

3.38 Antibiotics   Answers: A D E
Antibiotics are often used to prevent infection in surgery. A short, sharp dosage is recommended (i.e. 1–3 doses given intravenously). Prolonged courses are not advantageous. The definitive treatment of an abscess is incision and drainage. Patients at high risk of infection during surgery require prophylactic antibiotics, for example, patients with prosthetic heart valves, rheumatic heart disease, etc.

Cefuroxime (a second-generation cephalosporin) is active against enterococci and is often used for prophylaxis in cholecystectomy. In colorectal surgery, the major risk of infection is due to bowel organisms, i.e. anaerobes; metronidazole is used for this. A cephalosporin is added for prophylaxis against aerobes.

3.39 Urinary catheter obstruction   Answers: C D E
The passage of a urinary catheter presents a risk of infection both on insertion and removal. Epithelial damage allows access for bacteria into the circulation and septicaemia can result.

Artificial prostheses are particularly at risk. It is thus very important to use aseptic technique.

Antibiotic cover (for example, gentamicin intramuscularly) can be used.

Trauma during insertion may cause urethral bleeding.

Trauma to the prostate gland can cause acute prostatitis.

Renal calculi and pyelonephritis are not a problem.

3.40 Hyperhidrosis   Answers: D E

Hyperhidrosis is excess sweating of the skin. It is a common complaint and can be very distressing when it occurs in the hands. It classically occurs in young women. The aetiology is unknown but it is thought to be excessive vasomotor activity via sympathetic nerves. Treatment includes:

- axillary skin excision – the hair bearing area containing sweat glands is removed as a thin layer of skin
- cervical sympathectomy is used to abolish palmar sweating; a recognized complication of this is Horner's syndrome
- lumbar sympathectomy is used to abolish sweating of the soles.

3.41 Pre-operative investigations   Answers: A B E

The urgent investigations required in large bowel obstruction are:

- full blood count
- urea and electrolytes
- creatinine
- chest X-ray
- ECG.

These are the minimum requirements to facilitate safe anaesthesia.

Sigmoidoscopy is unlikely to alter the management.

A barium enema would cause delay. Laparotomy would still be required to relieve the obstruction.

3.42 Pseudomembranous colitis   Answers: B C D

Pseudomembranous colitis is colitis due to antibiotic therapy. Clindamycin was one of the first antibiotics to be implicated but cephalosporin therapy is more common. Pseudomembranous colitis is caused by an overgrowth of *Clostridium difficile*. It causes a profound watery diarrhoea and the formation of a membrane on the intestinal mucosa. Investigation is by:

- sigmoidoscopy and biopsy
- detection of *Clostridium difficile* toxin in the stool
- culture of *Clostridium difficile* from the stool.

Treatment is oral metronidazole or oral vancomycin.

3.43 Post-operative complications in 12 hours
Answers: A C D E

In the first 12 hours after an operation, the complications are those due to anaesthesia and those due to the surgery.
Complications of anaesthesia include:

- drug reactions or side effects
- trauma to the mouth or throat
- post-operative nausea and vomiting

- fluid imbalance; a fluid chart is essential to monitor fluid input and output; bowel surgery causes loss of large amounts of fluid and hypovolaemia may result; this predisposes to acute renal failure; if excess fluid is given, cardiac failure may occur due to overloading
- hypothermia – this does occur in bowel surgery where fluid loss is high and operations are long
- lung atelectasis/aspiration; hypoxia may result and therefore attention must be paid to oxygenation.

Complications of surgery include:

- reactionary haemorrhage.

Wound drainage is used to monitor any internal blood loss. (See also Paper 2, Question 41.)

3.44 Total parenteral nutrition (TPN)   Answers: B D
TPN is intravenous feeding.

Enteral nutrition is feeding via the gastrointestinal tract.

TPN is indicated for malnourished patients in whom the gastrointestinal tract is not functioning, for example, in obstruction.

Pre-operatively, TPN is beneficial to patients who are severely malnourished, i.e. only about 5% of patients.

Post-operatively, TPN is beneficial in malnourished patients as it improves wound healing and is required to overcome the catabolic phase.

TPN solutions have high osmolalities and are therefore

highly thrombophlebitic. They are therefore given via a central venous line into large veins where blood flow is high. The risks of central venous line insertion include haemorrhage, pneumothorax, air embolism and sepsis.

Enteral feeding is usually given via a fine bore nasogastric tube. If this is not tolerated, a percutaneous endoscopic gastrostomy (PEG) can be used.

3.45 Rectal bleeding   Answers: A B D
Bleeding *per rectum* occurs in:

- diverticulitis
- carcinoma of the rectum or colon
- haemorrhoids
- Meckel's diverticulum
- intussusception
- colitis where blood and mucus are seen
- melaena – old dark blood from peptic ulceration.

Intussusception occurs when a segment of bowel 'telescopes' into the adjacent section. It is most common before the age of two years. Ileo-caecal intussusception is the most common form. It presents with bowel obstruction; blood *per rectum* is described as 'redcurrant jelly stool' and is pathognomonic. The management is urgent barium enema which confirms the diagnosis and may even relieve the intussusception; if not, laparotomy is required.

Carcinoma of the oesophagus presents with faecal occult blood, but not blood on digital examination.

3.46 Thyroid carcinoma   Answers: A B D

Thyroid carcinoma is divided into four types:

- papillary
- follicular
- anaplastic
- medullary.

Papillary carcinoma affects children and young adults, females more than males. It presents as a slow growing lump. It is slow to spread and does so via lymphatics. It may therefore present with enlargement of lymph nodes. It moves on swallowing and is not fixed to the skin. There is an association with previous radiation. The standard treatment is total thyroidectomy. Prognosis is excellent.

Follicular carcinoma affects adults aged 40–50 years. It spreads via the bloodstream to lungs and bones and may therefore present with shortness of breath or bone pain. Treatment is thyroid lobectomy; if metastases are present total thyroidectomy is performed.

Anaplastic tumours present in older patients aged 60–80 years. It is more common in females than males. Spread is rapid. Patients present with a hard thyroid lump and symptoms of local invasion, such as hoarseness, if the recurrent laryngeal nerve is affected, or stridor, if the trachea is compressed. Prognosis is worse in this type. Surgical treatment is palliative.

Medullary carcinoma is a well-differentiated carcinoma of parafollicular cells which secrete calcitonin. It affects patients aged 50–70 years. Treatment is total thyroidectomy.

Thyroid carcinomas usually do NOT cause thyroid dys-function. Patients are often euthyroid.

3.47 Transplant surgery   Answers: B C D E

Renal transplantation has increased in numbers and success. It is used for patients in chronic renal failure and end-stage renal failure. Consideration is given to the patient's condition; patients over the age of 50 years are not excluded.

Transfer of tissue (for example, skin from one part of the body to another) is termed an *autograft;* from person to person is termed an *allograft;* from one species to another is termed a *xenograft.*

Rejection is due to the presence of antibodies and is a major problem.

Prevention is by tissue typing and immunosuppression.

Any infection must be treated prior to surgery.

3.48 Bowel stricture   Answers: B C D

Bowel stricture is due to a local inflammatory response.

The causes include:

- diverticular disease
- neoplasia
- Crohn's disease
- mesenteric ischaemia
- slow release potassium tablets.

Peutz–Jeghers syndrome is a cause of intestinal polyposis.

3.49 Amylase   Answers: A C D E

A marked rise in serum amylase occurs in acute pancreatitis (>1200 IU/ml). However, the level is not indicative of severity. Other causes include:

- diabetic ketoacidosis
- perforated peptic ulcer (not >600 IU/ml)
- acute cholecystitis
- renal failure
- strangulated bowel.

Acute appendicitis does not cause raised amylase.

3.50 Volvulus   Answers: A B C

Volvulus is the twisting of bowel. It usually occurs in the elderly and presents with abdominal distension and pain. Constipation may also be present. Complications are venous infarction or perforation resulting in peritonitis.

Investigations include:

- plain abdominal X-ray which shows a dilated bowel – sigmoid colon is usually affected and has an inverted horseshoe appearance.

Treatment is:

- insertion of a flatus tube
- barium enema without preparation
- surgery: laparotomy, sigmoid colectomy.

RECOMMENDED READING LIST

An Introduction to the Signs and Symptoms of Surgical Disease, Browse N, 3rd edition, Edward Arnold, 1997.

Essential Surgery – Problems, Diagnosis and Management, Burkett et al., 2nd edition, Churchill Livingstone, 1995.

Lecture Notes in General Surgery, Ellis and Calne, 8th edition, Blackwell Scientific, 1993.

Surgical Finals: Passing the Clinical, Kuperberg and Lumley, PasTest, 1996.

REVISION INDEX

The numbers after each item refer to the examination and question number.

Abdominal pain 2.25
Abcess,
   ischiorectal 2.48
   subphrenic 1.30
Achalasia 1.6
Adenoma, pleomorphic 1.47
Adenomatous polyposis,
   familial 2.3
Alkalosis, metabolic 1.26
Ampulla of Vater 1.10
Amylase 1.11, 3.49
Anaemia, iron deficiency 2.1
Anaesthesia 3.43
Anal fissure 2.33
Aneurysm,
   aortic 1.45
   congenital 1.45
Antibiotics 3.38
Appendicitis, acute 1.32
Arterial disease, peripheral 3.31
Artery, coronary 3.26
Atherosclerosis 1.21

Bell's palsy 1.33
Bile ducts 3.12
Bilirubin 1.11, 2.11
Bleeding, rectal 3.45
Blocking agents,
   neuromuscular 1.36
Bowel, stricture of 3.48
Buerger's disease 2.31
Burns 1.19
Burr hole 2.18

Caisson disease 3.25
Calcium 2.50
Calculi,
   renal 3.16
   ureteric 2.46

Cancer,
   basal cell 2.23
   breast 1.14, 2.14
   colon 3.9
   colo-rectal 1.3
   follicular 3.46
   oesophageal 1.49, 3.13
   papillary 3.46
   prostate 1.40
   stomach 1.37, 2.45
   thyroid 3.46
   tongue 3.33
Carbuncle 3.23
Carpal tunnel syndrome 2.34
Cartilage 1.34
Catheters, urinary 1.16, 3.39
Cellulitis 2.42
Chest injury 1.18
Cholecystitis, acute 1.50, 3.10
Cholangiopancreatography,
   retrograde endoscopic
   (ERCP) 1.9
Cholangitis, ascending 3.12
Cimetidine 2.36
Circle of Willis 2.32
Claudication, intermittent 1.21
Clostridium difficile 3.42
Clubbing 3.4
Colic, renal 2.25
Colitis, pseudo membranous 3.42
Colonoscopy 2.9
Complications, post-operative
   3.43
Constipation 2.6
Craniotomy 2.18
Crepitus 3.28
Crest syndrome 2.21
Crohn's disease 2.4, 2.9, 2.38,
   3.4

CT scan 3.13
Cystinuria 2.46, 3.16
Cysts 1.13, 2.13, 2.16

Defaecation 3.24
Diabetes mellitus 3.31
Diarrhoea 1.29
Diuretic 2.41
Diverticular disease 3.7, 3.9
Ducts, bile 3.12
Dumping syndrome 1.29
Dupuytren's contracture 2.39
Dysphagia 3.6, 3.13

Echinococcus granulosus 2.12
Ehlers–Danlos syndrome 1.45
Embolism 3.21
Embolus,
    arterial 3.25
    mesenteric 2.5
Emphysema 3.28
Empyema 3.10
Endoscopic retrograde
    cholangiopancreatography
    (ERCP) 1.9
Enema, barium 3.9
Epithelium 3.3
Escherichia coli 3.10

Faeces 2.48
Fracture, compound 2.35
Femur 2.40
Fibroadenoma 3.14
Fibroadenosis 1.43
Fibrocystic disease 1.43
Fissure, anal 2.48, 3.24
Fistula, recurrent 2.24
Fractures,
    femoral shaft 2.40
    femur, intertrochanteric 3.37
Frusemide 2.41

Gag reflex 1.46
Gallstones 1.10, 2.10
Gangrene, 3.21
    gas 1.42
Gastrectomy, post- 1.29
Gastroscopy 2.28
Gastrointestinal bleed 2.28
Gaucher's disease 1.35
Gout 2.46
Gynaecomastia 1.44

H_2-antagonists 2.36
Haematemesis 2.28, 3.15
Haematoma,
    extradural 2.18
Haematuria 1.17, 3.17
Haemorrhage,
    extradural 2.18
    internal 3.15
Haemorrhoids 1.7, 2.7
Helicobacter pylori 2.2
Heparin 3.36
Hepatitis B 3.11
Hernia,
    femoral 1.8, 2.8, 3.8
    hiatus 1.1
    inguinal 3.19
Hodgkin's disease 2.4
Horner's syndrome 1.31
Hydatid disease 2.12
Hydrocoele 2.15, 2.16
Hyperhidrosis 3.40
Hyperparathyroidism 2.37, 2.46
Hypocalcaemia 1.22, 2.50
Hypotension 1.28
Hypovolaemia 1.28

Investigations,
    pre-operative 3.41
Ischaemia 2.5
Ischaemic heart disease 3.26

Jaundice, obstructive 1.11, 2.11

Krukenberg tumours 1.37

Laparotomy 3.41
Lipoma 3.14
Lumbar disc, prolapsed 3.34
Lump, breast 3.14
Lumpectomy 2.49
Lymphoedema 1.14
Lymph nodes 2.13

Mammography 2.49
Mandible 2.13
Marfan's syndrome 1.45
Meckel's diverticulum 1.5, 2.37, 2.43
Melanoma,
    malignant 1.23, 2.30, 3.30
Meniscus, medial tears 1.34
Metastases, bone 3.35
Myocardial infarction 1.28

Nasogastric tube 1.46
Necrosis, avascular 1.42, 1.35
Nephrectomy 3.17
Nissen's fundoplication 1.1

Obstruction,
    renal 1.17
    small bowel 1.5
    ureteric 1.15
Oesophagus 2.1
Oesophagogastroduodenoscopy
    3.13
Oliguria,
    post-operative 2.41

Paget's disease 1.14
Palmar fascia 2.39
Pancreatitis, acute 1.22, 2.22, 2.50

Paralytic ileus 1.48, 3.5
Parenteral nutrition,
    total (TPN) 3.44
Peau d'orange 3.14
Peritoneum 1.8
Perthe's disease 1.35
Peutz–Jeghers syndrome 3.3
Pharynx 2.13
Polyps,
    colonic 3.3
    pseudo 3.18
Processus vaginalis 2.15
Pruritus 3.24
Pyrexia 1.32

Ranitidine 2.36
Raynaud's phenomenon 2.21, 3.21
Reflux,
    acid 1.1
    gastro-oesophageal 2.1
Renal failure, acute 2.17

Salivary duct, calculi of 2.44
Salivary glands 1.47
Sarcoma 1.39
Scrotum 2.16
Septicaemia 2.50, 3.10
Sinus, pilonidal 2.29
Spleen, 1.12
    rupture of 3.15
Steatorrhea 2.38
Stenosis, carotid artery 2.32
Surgery,
    invasive 1.38
    laparoscopic 1.38

Telangiectasia 2.23
Testis, undescended 2.19
Tetany 2.26
Thrombus 3.21

Thrombosis,
    deep vein 3.27
Toe nail, ingrowing 2.27
Total parenteral nutrition (TPN)
    3.44
Transplantation, renal 3.47
Trauma, metabolic response to
    2.47
Troisier's sign 2.45
Tuberculosis 3.32
Tumour,
    anaplastic 3.46
    breast 2.49

Ulcer,
    duodenal 1.2, 3.2
    gastric 2.2, 3.2
    Marjolin's 3.20
    peptic 2.37, 3.2
    rodent 2.23
Ulcerative colitis 1.4, 2.38, 3.1,
    3.4, 3.18
Urine, dark 2.11
Urogram, intravenous 1.15

Variococele 1.17, 2.20
Varicose veins 1.20
Virchow's node 2.45
Vitamins 3.4
Volvulus 3.50
Vomiting 1.22, 1.26, 3.2

Wound 1.27

X-ray, chest 2.9, 3.9, 3.26

Zollinger–Ellison syndrome 2.37

PASTEST REVISION BOOKS

PasTest are the specialists in study guides and revision courses for professional medical qualifications. For 25 years we have been helping doctors to achieve their potential. The new PasTest range of books for medical students includes:

OSCEs for Medical Undergraduates — Volume 1
Feather, Visvanathan & Lumley (ISBN 1 901198 04 9)
OSCEs for Medical Undergraduates — Volume 2
Visvanathan, Feather & Lumley (ISBN 1 901198 05 7)
- Covers history-taking, examinations, investigations, practical techniques, making a diagnosis, prescribing treatment and other issues
- Each chapter includes questions from each type of OSCE station

Surgical Finals: Passing the Clinical
Kuperberg & Lumley (ISBN 0 906896 38 X)
Medical Finals: Passing the Clinical
Moore & Richardson (ISBN 0 906896 43 6)
- 100 typical long and short clinical cases
- Syllabus checklists for systematic revision
- Structured examination plans for all cases

Surgical Finals: Structured Answer & Essay Questions
Visvanathan & Lumley (ISBN 0 906896 69 X)
Medical Finals: Structured Answer & Essay Questions
Feather, Visvanathan & Lumley (ISBN 0 906896 79 7)
- Unique combination of essay questions and the new SAQs
- Sample essays and model essay plans
- Revision checklists to track your progress

150 Essential MCQs for Surgical Finals
Hassanally & Singh (ISBN 1 901198 01 4)
150 Essential MCQs for Medical Finals
Singh & Hassanally (ISBN 1 901198 02 2)
- The crucial material for your exam success
- Extended teaching notes, bullet points and mnemonics
- Revision indexes for easy access to specific topics

All PasTest books are available from good bookshops or contact us directly to order your books by mail. All orders are despatched within 24 hours. See the Order Form overleaf.

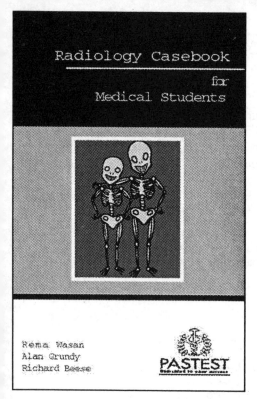